C A Stauffacher

ALOIS LANG, SCULPTOR, THE CHRIST FOR 1930

The Passion Play of Oberammergau

ITS HISTORY AND SIGNIFICANCE

By
JANET H. M. SWIFT, M.A.

ILLUSTRATED

NEW YORK   CHICAGO
Fleming H. Revell Company
LONDON AND EDINBURGH

Printed in the United States of America

New York: 158 Fifth Avenue
Chicago: 851 Cass Street
London: 21 Paternoster Square
Edinburgh: 99 George Street

*To the memory of the gallant Captain,
seventy-five years young, and the gentle
Birthday Lady, whose seventy-third natal
day was devoted to the Passion Play of
twenty years ago, the Scribe of this year
of Our Lord 1930 dedicates the following
rominiscence and narrative.*

FOREWORD

"So pricketh hem Nature in her corages,
Than longen folk to gon on pilgrimages."
—CHAUCER.

AGAIN the Passion Play—again the great summer pilgrimage to the little village in the Bavarian Alps! For Oberammergau beckons, and the world responds. As the weeks pass, almost every ship leaving an American port will carry its quota of pilgrims to join with similar companies, hailing from the continent of Europe, from the far East, the North, and the South, in search of their common goal, this tiny village in the Bavarian Alps.

Over land and sea the pilgrims will come—by foot, by caravan, by rail, by automobile, through the air. They will come, too, with varying motives—deep reverence, as to a shrine; careless curiosity, as to a show; calm indifference, as to a mere pastime; earnest interest, as to an absorbing study; superficial sentiment, as to a thrilling spectacle; eager anticipation, as to a long-looked-for pleasure; solemn expectancy, as to a very fount of blessing. In these varied attitudes of mind will come, young and old, rich and poor,

7

peasant and king, schoolboy and professor, layman and priest. Mental acumen, business sagacity, social leadership, ignorant zeal, unquestioning loyalty—all these will be drawn by the magnetism of the Cross on the Kofel, towering above the peaceful mountain village. Truly all roads will lead to Oberammergau during the summer of 1930!

And *Why?* To offer an answer to this query and to attempt an explanation of this phenomenon, is the plan and purpose of this little volume.

Many sources have contributed to the information contained herein, but special mention should be made of the delightful and intimate account of the village in the book *Oberammergau*, written by Mrs. Louise Parks-Richards in 1910. This has been largely the authority for the spelling of the village names, and for various items of a personal nature.

J. H. M. S.

CONTENTS

PART ONE
THE PLACE AND ITS PEOPLE

PART TWO
THE PLAY AND THE PLAYERS

ADDENDA

PART ONE

THE PLACE AND ITS PEOPLE

I

INTRODUCTORY

IT was one of life's memorable days! As one
looks backward over years that are past, one
finds that the really memorable days, golden
days which glow persistently in the memory, while
fondly cherished, are comparatively few.

Such a day in the life of the writer was August
8, 1910—the day given to the Passion Play in
Oberammergau. It was not an incident, it was an
experience—one never to be forgotten. It was not
a spectacle, it was an influence—one destined to
last, through all the days that were to come.

Among the throngs boarding the train at Munich
for the trip to Oberammergau on August 7, 1910,
were three persons whom we propose to call the
Captain, seventy-five years young, the gentle
Birthday Lady—was she not looking forward to
the following day as her seventy-third birthday,
and was she not to celebrate it in a wholly unique
manner?—and the present writer in the rôle of
general guide and attendant.

We left Munich at 1:20 P. M. for Oberammergau, and memory recalls the feeling of expectancy
and interest which grew steadily during the three

hours' ride (uphill all the way) into the beautiful Ammer Valley, rich with yellow grain dotted with scarlet poppies, which led past the romantic shores of the Starnberg See (pointed out as the watery grave of the unfortunate Ludwig II.), through picturesque villages and wild mountain gorges, until we were borne into the billowing bosom of the Bavarian Alps and saw, nestling in a peaceful valley, the goal of our quest—the village of Oberammergau.

Leaving the train, we find ourselves on a long, open platform at one end of the town whose main street stretches out before us.

A Tyrolean cab-driver garbed in picturesque costume—short leather trousers, heavy woolen hose, reaching from ankle to knee, short coat and shirt criss-crossed with bands of vivid embroidery, and little peaked hat adorned with either flower or feather—greets us with his welcome *"Grüsz Gott,"* and induces us to climb into his heavy old-fashioned cab. The horse, hitched on one side of the tongue of the vehicle and monotonously jingling the bell he wears about his neck, proceeds very slowly up the street.

As we move along, eagerly scanning the novel sights that present themselves, we are impressed with the dazzling whiteness of the village houses, the river flowing through the town, the flowers which are everywhere. We see evidences that we are expected, too, for booths along the street announce "American Ice Cream," and that English " is spoke," while the barber boldly advertises his " Champoon." At the centre of the town we come upon the village drinking fountain, the post office, and a number of interesting little shops with their tempting contents.

We leave our cab to find ourselves in a curious labyrinth of narrow, irregular streets leading off in every direction. The houses seem to have been dropped down, hit or miss, and we wind in and out among them, running into cowshed or front door just as the case may happen to be.

We wander through shady lanes, we glimpse the really fine church with its queer mosque-like tower —it is the centre of the life of the village—and we have our first view of the great theatre, the object of our special interest. But evening draws on, and we have the interesting experience before us of visiting the busy Wohnungsbureau, and finding our host. The Captain, seventy-five years young and ready for adventure, rejoices exceedingly, and makes prompt friends with a Pharisee—so we discover, and Samuel by name—a tall, bearded man in picturesque attire: knee-breeches, dark cape carelessly thrown over one shoulder and slouch hat, resting upon his dark flowing locks. With stately mien and solemn tread, he looks over our baggage and guides us to his home. Here we find his buxom daughter and pleasant wife, who provide for us in as kindly a fashion as though we

were really guests. They quite captivate the
gentle Birthday Lady, who is much interested in
the long, low living-room, with its tile stove and
decorations of mounted animal-heads on the walls;
in the tiny bedrooms, with their narrow beds and
huge feather pillows and coverlets; in the well-
equipped kitchen with its cabinet of dishes on the
wall and large cook-stove, from the interior recesses of which (instead of from the top) a vessel
of hot water is produced at our request. Good
food is provided for us—the best bit of beefsteak
we were to encounter in a whole summer's trip—
and the meal is spread on a pleasant porch overlooking a beautiful garden. So we find ourselves
in the heart of Oberammergau, and amid the peace
and comfort of this kindly home, we seek our first
night's repose.

At five o'clock the next morning we are awakened by a melodious peal of bells, and again at six,
the chimes announce that the day of days has
arrived. Seven forty-five finds us well provided
with maps, text-books, opera-glasses, and great
square leather cushions which will prove so ac-
ceptable before the long day's sitting is over. We
approach the theatre, to find that from every direction our comrades are coming—coming, from every
corner of the earth. They seem to be almost rising out of the ground, and all going in one direction. But it is an orderly crowd actuated by a
serious purpose. There is little confusion; every

seat is numbered, plans are well carried out, and
in a comparatively short space of time, the vast
audience is settled in its place.

How shall I describe that silently waiting audience? Many Americans are in evidence, and repre-
sentatives of almost all other nations and races
are there, but Germans predominate. I am impressed with the number of men present, and there
is a generous sprinkling of priests. It is an unusually orderly group of four thousand people,
waiting with eager expectancy for the first notes
from an orchestra hidden in a recess. At exactly
eight o'clock, the silence is broken, and for the
rest of the day we are lost to the world—a great
company of souls lifted and carried with the Christ
along the *Via Dolorosa,* the Sorrowful Way, into
the gloom of Gethsemane and out into the light of
the Resurrection. We may react later (though
after this experience we shall never be quite the
same), but for the time being, we are held spellbound by a marvellous portrayal, and are followers of the Christ—ready to exclaim with the late
William T. Stead:

"This is the story that transformed the world!
This is the story that transformed the world!
Yes, and will yet transform it!
Yes, thank God, so the answer comes, and will yet
transform it, until Thy Kingdom comes! "

II

OBERAMMERGAU

THE name borne by this Bavarian village
is rapidly becoming a household word
throughout the civilized world, much as
Bethlehem and Calvary have been, for nineteen
centuries. Literally, the word means the " ober "
or upper of two villages, situated in the " gau " or
region of the river Ammer. There is also Unter—
lower—Ammergau, a few miles distant.

The place itself is a picturesque mountain village, located in a level valley in the midst of the
Bavarian Alps, near the southernmost boundary
of the German Republic. "As the mountains are
round about Jerusalem " so are the hills about
Oberammergau, in the bosom of which it nestles
and looks up and off to the snow-capped peaks
beyond.

The Oberammergau district includes the Ammer
Mountains, and the Ammer Valley through which
the river flows. The mountains are mostly of the
rounded variety, with magnificent forests of pine
and fir which subside into grassy slopes and terraces overgrown with gaily-coloured flowers.

At the southeast of the village is grand old

THE HANSEL AND GRETEL HOUSE AT OBERAMMERGAU, SHOWING
PAINTING ON THE WALLS

(This and all the other illustrations in this volume are used by courtesy of the German
Tourist Information Office, N. Y.)

Laber, consisting of solid marble and rising to a
height of five thousand five hundred feet—a great
natural rampart for the protection of the village.
The special guardian of the community is the
Kofel—a sentinel-crag which forms the eastern
pillar of the Sonnenberg ridge. This peak, ab-
rupt and clear cut, rises two thousand feet above
the valley, and figures largely in the life of the
village. It is said to have been known to the
Romans, and, in the Middle Ages, betrothals were
celebrated upon its summit. From the earliest
Christian times a large wooden cross has been
erected upon it, which the villagers reverence and
renew as time and decay render necessary.

The Ammer flows down from the mountains
through the valley, and through some of the
streets of the village, where it is crossed by little
bridges. Here, the housewife may stand to do her
washing in the village washtub, as the river is
called. The Ammer formerly submerged the valley in an annual flood, but the progressive natives
of Oberammergau, with funds derived from their
Passion Play, have applied themselves most intel-
ligently to the problem, widening and straightening the refractory river so that, now, it peacefully
waters the valley, and gives the villagers fertile
fields for agricultural purposes, and rich meadow-
land for grazing.

The altitude of the village itself is two thousand
five hundred feet above sea level, and the climate

is salubrious, both in winter and summer. According to the village doctor, the place is "disgustingly healthy." It is coming to be a health resort, very beneficial for nerve and heart affections. It is sheltered from the winds by surrounding mountains, and is of comparatively even temperature, with much blue sky and sunshine. The wealth also of forest—pine and fir, beech, elm, and maple—imparts a tonic to the atmosphere.

It is a fine region for winter sports. One of the principal Passion Play actors introduced the sport of skiing which, at first, afforded great amusement to his fellow-villagers. Snowshoeing and tobogganing, too, are popular in the mountains and foothills.

Oberammergau is especially equipped for the care of tourists, and prices are very reasonable except, possibly, during the Passion Play season, when the great demand necessarily and naturally makes for increased prices.

This little village of about two thousand inhabitants, is able to offer, at least, four thousand five hundred beds to its guests, and, without exception, the houses are built for the accommodation of the decennial crowds. It is a most interesting village, well kept, and, at least every ten years, shining with new white paint and plaster. The houses are numbered consecutively, beginning at one end of the town and continuing to the other, but no order or regularity has been followed in the laying-out of the streets. In fact, the whole place is a curious labyrinth, especially in the central part. On this account alone, it is most picturesque, and there are gardens and window-boxes and shaded lanes to render it the more interesting.

The style of architecture also is characteristic—low, commodious houses with broad, overhanging roofs covered with red tile, or in the instance of some of the older ones, with loose shingles dotted with heavy stones to keep the former from blowing away in the winter storms. The houses have heavy wooden shutters, and many of them are covered with white plaster decorated with frescoes representing Biblical and mythological scenes. Some of these paintings are two hundred years old, and reveal the characteristic artistry of the Middle Ages.

Some of the real peasant's houses have the stable sheltered under the same roof as the family dwelling; but even in these, are rooms spotlessly clean and reserved for Passion Play guests, the family cow being accommodated in quarters adjoining. There are also numbers of well-built, attractive houses provided with every conceivable comfort. Such an one is the house of Anton Lang, rendered doubly attractive by overhanging vines and beautiful garden. It is called "The Pension Daheim," and provides for the entertainment of tourists at all seasons of the year. Many people recall with pleasure their stay in the hospitable house of the *Christus* of the Passion Play. Other good pensions and hotels offer comfortable rooms, sanitary equipment and wholesome food, where, moreover, host and hostess welcome their guests as friends, and care for them with an interest so hearty and spontaneous as almost to eliminate any thought of the actual relationship which exists between that of a common tourist and the people of his temporary sojourn.

The Oberammergau stores compel notice. Such curiosity shops! Such wonderful variety and range of artistic objects! Such an unusual exhibit of village handicrafts! Of course, wood carvings and pottery prevail, but sculpture, painting, engraving, and textile weaving all are shown in great profusion. The smaller shops fairly bulge with curios of all kinds and descriptions, including the ubiquitous picture postcard of an unusually fine quality.

The village drinking-fountain is located in the square near the post-office, and possesses considerable interest. Here congregate villagers and guests, young and old, to discuss the news of the day. Heretofore, the village forge has been a magnet which attracts visitors, who find in Hugo Rutz, the village smith, a most genial man and lively conversationalist. He has a welcome for all at his smithy, as he labours at his craft between the sessions of the Passion Play, in which he supports the important rôle of *Caiaphas*.

The institution of which, probably, the village is most proud is the School of Wood Carving. This

is a large and modern building equipped to give
the young people of the village expert instruction
in the noble art of wood carving, for which Oberammergau would surely be famous, even though
she had not her Passion Play. This school has
been under the direction of Ludwig Lang and
Anton Lechner, and it augurs well for the future
of the village that so many of its youth are to be
found working so eagerly at the peaceful arts of
carving, moulding, and modelling.

The centre and inspiration of the life of Oberammergau, as of other such communities the world
over, is, and has always been, the Church. An
unusually fine building here testifies to the place
it occupies in the regard of the people. With its
tall, mosque-like tower it is visible throughout the
valley, and adorns one end of the village as the
great theatre does the other. It has an harmonious chime of bells and some really fine stained
glass. As might be expected, the interior contains
some wonderful carving—a beautiful communion-
rail and some richly decorated altars. There is
also a splendid organ, presented to the community
by some English friends, after the Passion Play
of 1890.

The churchyard is a spot of sacred memories to
the people, and the monuments of their dead leaders are shrines, around which, each Sunday after
Mass, they gather in devotion. The beautiful
monument to the sons of the village who fell in

the Franco-Prussian War is here, as is a memorial
to the teacher who composed the Passion music.
The finest of these monuments is that of the great
teacher and friend, the good Father Daisenberger,
to whom, more than to any one man, the Passion
Play owes its present form. One of the final acts
of the Passion Play season, in which the actors
engage, ere dispersing and reëntering their normal
lives and occupations, is the processional which is
made to pass the bronze bust of this spiritual
father for so many years, and to do him honour
and reverence.

The building of chief interest in Oberammergau
is the great theatre. It was built for the Play of
1900, at a cost of about fifty thousand dollars,
and paid for from the receipts of the Play of that
year. It is built on six great iron arches, each with
a span of one hundred and forty feet, and a height
of sixty-five feet. To these the roof and walls of
wood are fastened, and the end facing the stage
is left open, so that the general effect is not unlike
that of a great railway shed. The exterior is covered with yellow canvas, and decorated with the
painted figures of saints and seers. At the corners
are carved figures of the prophets. There are fourteen entrances and the auditorium is built to seat
four thousand people. During the past year, the
village has been bonded in order to realize the
necessary funds to rebuild and enlarge the seating
capacity of the auditorium to five thousand. The

seats slope upward quite abruptly, so that there is a good view of the stage from every seat, and the acoustic properties of the auditorium are perfect.

At the rear are the royal boxes, royalty from many countries being attracted hither. On the wall on either side of the boxes the scenes of the first Passion Play are painted, together with some views of the monastery of Ettal, so closely connected with it from the very beginning. As previously stated, the end of the theatre facing the stage is open, and the stage itself is entirely uncovered. It is claimed for it, that it is the largest in the world, easily accommodating seven hundred performers at once, and that without crowding. It consists of four parts; the proscenium, with steps at each end leading to the house of Annas, at the right as one faces the stage, and to the house of Pilate, which is at the left. Here the great multitudes gather for the Triumphal Entry and other crowded scenes.

The central stage is really a separate building or pavilion, and here the interior scenes are presented and the wonderful tableaux staged. The front is covered by a drop screen, on which is painted Michael Angelo's Moses, with Isaiah and Jeremiah on each side. The screen opens crosswise, one half sliding up and the other down, disclosing a curtain which is drawn apart from the centre. Light is introduced through a skylight in the roof.

On each side of this central pavilion are wide-

open spaces leading to the proscenium, which is
decorated with plants and vine-covered walls, sup-
posedly representing the streets of Jerusalem.
Here, under the open sky and in view of real
mountain scenery, the Play proceeds hour after
hour, without regard to wind or weather. If the
storm be unusually severe, a brief wait may be
arranged, and the chorus permitted to change to
its second best robes. Sometimes, it is said, the
changing weather conditions add greatly to the
effect, as when the elements rage during the Crucifixion, or the sunlight suddenly shines forth,
making a halo over the head of *Christus*—phenomena which are said to have really occurred.

The area behind the stage is of great interest.
Twenty-three rooms are required to form a re-
freshment room for the use of the actors, dressing-
rooms, and many rooms for the various properties
—a thousand costumes, hundreds of pairs of san-
dals, a room full of Roman spears, helmets and
shields, the dainty garments for the angels in the
tableaux, the simple shepherd robes for the disciples, the gorgeous gowns of the scribes and Pharisees—a very storehouse of Oriental splendour.

Truly a village of unusual features is this
modern Mecca, and one to which tourists will continue to be drawn. But there are other interesting
villages in Bavaria, and Oberammergau must present some further claims in order to explain the
Why of the great summer pilgrimage.

III

APPROACH AND ENVIRONS

IN nine cases out of ten, the village of Oberammergau is approached from Munich, a
distance of about sixty-five miles. At any
season of the year it is a beautiful ride, whether
made by rail or motor. In the autumn, the glory
of the scene is beyond description. It is uphill all
the way—the route leading past romantic lakes
almost hidden by wooded shores, past haunting
ravines, grassy moors, quaint farmhouses, enchant-
ing villas. The mountains, growing higher and
wrapping you around, point with up-reaching,
rocky fingers to the sunclad peaks beyond, or open
their doors to disclose picturesque little villages
nestling in their arms. At Murnau, steam is exchanged for electricity, and one enters a peaceful
valley, watered by a swift-flowing, trout-filled
stream, which holds in its lap the rambling,
glistening, colourful village of Oberammergau.

If, however, the journey be entered upon from
the south, or from Switzerland, the route will probably start from Innsbrück by way of those twin
mountain gems, Garmisch and Partenkirchen. In
this instance, the grandeur of the Alps is at the

beginning of the trip, at the very foot of the
Zugspitze, the highest peak in Germany, with an
altitude of upwards of nine thousand six hundred
feet, to the summit of which a " ground railway "
has recently been built at a cost of four million
dollars. From this point the route leads through
picturesque, rather than sublime, natural scenery,
into the charming foothills and wooded terraces
of the Ammer Valley, where the much-sought
village lies.

The immediate surroundings of Oberammergau
offer some delightful walks, which even the newly
initiated may enjoy. There are shady lanes, and
paths which lead through the leafy forests, with
gentle streams to cross and occasional glimpses of
stag or chamois. There is an abundance of wild
flowers—rare Alpine plants—and a wealth of
cryptogams. Convenient benches offer welcome
resting-places, and, here and there, a wayside
shrine, with its crucifix or little chapel, directs
attention to the Giver of this wealth of natural
beauty, and invites worship and praise. There are
regularly planned walks of various lengths suited
to different grades of pedestrian endurance, and
from them all, in every direction, some phase of
natural beauty meets the eye—now the grandeur
of a mountain-top, or the wonder of some vast,
rocky crag; there, the peace of flowing river; yon-
der, the dark mystery of unexplored forest; here,
the delicate beauty of the blossom underfoot. The

local Improvement Society has exercised much commonsense and artistic skill in laying out these pleasant walks with their quiet resting-places, in particularly attractive spots, where the views are especially fine. An easy walk is to the Rainebichl, where from a pavilion one may feast his eyes on a charming view of the village and valley. The walk to St. Gregor is along the banks of the Leine, a wild, little mountain stream, and back through the green meadows to the Passion Play theatre. Another interesting walk is over the Lourdes-Grotto, an artificial stalactite cave cut into the rock, where a small lamp burns eternally, before a statue of the Madonna of Lourdes.

The really strenuous pedestrian finds himself right in his element, for there are mountain walks and mountain climbs varying in time-length from an afternoon to a day, or even two. The Kofel is a favourite climb, and considered an easy one, although more accidents have happened on it than on many a more difficult Alpine climb, because of steep declivities and projecting patches of grass, hiding unsafe rocky walls. The ascent takes an hour and a half, and the view is most rewarding, the whole valley being spread out in beauteous, colourful panorama. The sound of the church bells reaches the ear, and human voices can be heard in the village below, although coming from the top of a practically perpendicular rock, two thousand feet above the level of the valley.

The Aufacher trip is another favourite. The ascent is about five thousand five hundred feet, and may be made comfortably, at night, in order to obtain a view of the sunrise the following morning. This is an indescribable sight—the surrounding peaks and mountain lakes gleaming in the morning glow, which precedes the appearance of the sun rising in his splendours, and flings its reflection to the farthest bounds of mountain and plain.

Other and more adventurous mountain trips, requiring the help of experienced guides, may be taken, according to the desire and the ability of the visitor.

One of the excursions which should not be omitted, is the trip to the monastery of Ettal, about three miles southeast of the village. This monastery possesses great interest as a mediæval institution, and also because of its intimate connection with Oberammergau from its earliest days. In fact, it is to this monastery, and to the village teachers and leaders it has furnished, that the village owes much of its peculiar character and accomplishments—wood carving, probably, and, more than likely, the Passion Play.

The monastery of Ettal dates back to the fourteenth century. The tradition holds that, in the year 1329, Ludwig IV. of Bavaria came up from Rome at the head of his army. He came by an old Roman highway, supposed to date back to the time of the days of Tiberius, and to have been, originally, a military road leading into the newly-conquered northern country, and a thousand years later, the trade thoroughfare between Italy and Germany.

Ludwig is said to have carried with him an alabaster figure of a Madonna and Child, given him by an angel from heaven. As he was journeying through the mountains, the image grew so heavy that his horse sank down three times to the ground. Believing this to be a sign from heaven, he vowed to build a monastery on the spot, and the following year, laid the foundations of the Church of Our Lady of Ettal. Later, the Madonna and Child was placed in the high altar of the church, where it has been retained, and venerated from that day to this, through many changes and vicissitudes. Only the outside walls of the structure built by King Ludwig are now standing, and there have been foreign inroads and confiscations, and serious fires. At one period of its history the church was converted into a brewery, with the inscription, " God Bless the Beer of Ettal," carved over one of its gateways. In later days, it was restored by the Benedictine monks, and has exercised a wonderful influence for good over the whole region round about.

The famous church is most picturesquely located in the midst of surrounding hills. It has an inspiring dome, and contains some paintings of value—*The Ascension of the Virgin Mary*, by Knoller, and five other altar pieces. The Benedictine altar is also very fine, but the Madonna of King Ludwig is the most cherished possession. Dismissing its miraculous origin, one may note that some authorities claim the beautiful transparent material of which it is wrought to be Indian porphyry, and assign it to an early Christian date, or even to a period before the coming of Christ. The figure is regarded as possessing great charm, the faces of both Mother and Child reflecting a deep spiritual expression.

Given a region of such unusual variety and beauty as the Bavarian Highlands, and, in Munich, hard by, a royal family duly appreciating the beautiful, and it is not to be wondered at that the whole region became the favourite recreation ground for princes of the blood. Large districts were reserved for royal hunting-grounds, where herds of stag and chamois were kept, and many hunting paths laid out through the forests. Here Luitpold, the Prince Regent, was fond of entertaining chamois-hunting parties. But the whole region is especially noted as being the special rendezvous of the so-called " mad king," Ludwig II.

The relations of this king-prince with the people of the Bavarian Highlands deserve something more than a mere note, furnishing, as they do, an instance of unusual loyalty and devotion. The sad life-story of Ludwig needs only to be touched upon. He came of a family devoted to art, his grandfather, Ludwig I., having made Munich one of the

art centres of the world. To the younger Ludwig is
due the honour of having saved the Wagnerian
operas for the pleasure and profit of future
generations.

A handsome, sensitive lad of artistic tempera-
ment, Ludwig was brought up with the greatest
severity, and left so much alone, that he became
subject to abnormal fancies and fantastic dreams.
To music and the drama he was passionately devoted. His chief companions were the subjects of
the paintings and sculpture in the royal Residenz
in Munich, and the Castle of Hohenschwangau,
where the art-loving family had assembled their
treasures. He became familiar with *Lohengrin* and
the other heroes of the Wagnerian compositions,
and cherished a consuming admiration for their
composer. Hence, one of his first acts, on becoming
king of Bavaria, was to bring Wagner to Munich.
It was at a time when the composer was the subject
of much adverse criticism, and the royal favour
meant new life for him. A great friendship sprang
up between the two men, which continued, although
the king's ministers forced Wagner's removal from
Munich, and prevented the building of the great
Festspiel Haus, which Ludwig had planned.

Opposed and humiliated, the king eventually
shut himself away from his ministers and family,
and lived almost as an exile in his royal castles in
the Bavarian Alps. He turned his artistic genius
into new channels and started a positive orgy of

building. Castle after castle was projected in the wildest, most inaccessible places, some of them being built and furnished with oriental magnificence. Ludwig lived in solitary grandeur, and rode through the mountain-passes at night, in a gorgeous chariot, attended by liveried attendants and outriders. But he made himself much beloved by the Bavarian mountaineers, who jealously thought of him as their own particular monarch. Especially was he attracted to Oberammergau, often visiting the village and making friends with its people, who followed him adoringly. It is related that, on Christmas Eve, 1871, he appeared in the village and visited the church, making his way to it from the edge of the village on foot. He inspected " die Krippe " (the representation of the Nativity), and knelt in prayer in the church. In the same year, he, with his retinue, took possession of the Passion Play theatre, and witnessed a special performance of the Play. In connection with this celebration, he invited the *Christus* and some of the other chief actors to dine with him at the beautiful castle of Linderhof. But alas, the *Judas* of the play had no black coat, and to his great distress was obliged to go in his everyday " joppe " (jacket). He hesitated to approach the king, but being reassured by an attendant, was soon engaged in such pleasant conversation with Ludwig, that his " joppe " and everything of a like nature was entirely forgotten.

Ludwig's real affection for the people of Ober-

OBERAMMERGAU, THE PASSION PLAY VILLAGE IN THE BAVARIAN ALPS

On the right is the Passion Play Theatre and the church can be seen on the left.

ammergau is perpetually witnessed to, by the gift
he made them. One of the chief points of interest
in the neighbourhood is the Ludwig monument. It
is erected on the highest point of the Osterbichl
Hills, lying on the outskirts of the village. In front
of the monument is a wide-open space, where, on
certain saints' days, and on the anniversary of
Ludwig's death, Mass is celebrated. The locality
commands a magnificent view of the village and
surrounding mountains, while the monument itself
is of imposing effect, being of Kelheim marble, and
forty feet in height. It represents a Crucifixion
group, with Mary and John at the foot of the
Cross. The inscription which Ludwig had en-
graved upon it reads as follows: " To the art
loving Oberammergauers, faithful to the customs
of their fathers, from King Ludwig II., in remembrance of the Passion Play."

The befogged mental condition of the unfortunate young monarch grew steadily worse, until he
ended his ill-starred career beneath the waters of
the neighbouring Starnberg See. His kingdom,
generally, mourned the untimely death of their
king, but his loyal devoted mountaineers were cast
into the deepest sorrow by the loss of their friend,
and cherish his memory with rare devotion.

Bavaria has more castles within a small radius
than probably any other country, and some of
them are easily visited from Oberammergau. Berg
Castle, on Lake Starnberg, is beautifully located,

and rich in souvenirs of the " Mad King," who
spent much time here. There is also a Roman-
esque memorial chapel erected on the shores of
the lake, in which he found his watery grave.
Hohenschwangau, the old family castle of Ludwig's childhood, was built by Maximilian II., in
1832. It is wonderfully situated, overlooking the
Alpsee, and contains some interesting frescoes il-
lustrating early Bavarian history and folklore.
Near this old castle, and on an almost inaccessible
rocky eminence, Ludwig built Neuschwanstein, in
1868. The interior is richly decorated with frescoes representing scenes from the Wagnerian
operas, while the Singers' Room and Throne Room
show architectural excellence of a high order. The
exquisite Linderhof Palace is a short drive from
Oberammergau, in the Graswang Valley. Ludwig
built this gem of a palace in 1875. It is surrounded
by extensive gardens, containing sculptures, terraces, and cascades. It is luxuriantly furnished
and in many of its features commemorates Ludwig's fondness for Wagner.

These are some of the unique attractions of the
mountain region which is felicitously called the
" Cradle of the Passion Play." Travellers come
from far to see such examples of art and gaze upon
such wonders of nature. But are these things
sufficiently potent to draw two hundred thousand
people into their midst during a short summer
season? Do *they* answer the *Why?*

IV

THE PEOPLE OF THE VILLAGE:
CHARACTERISTICS

WE have glanced at some of the interesting features of this modern Mecca in the Bavarian Alps, and have seen that the little village and its environs are marked by rare natural attractions, and contain many evidences of the high ideals and human skill of the dwellers therein; but these, alone, fail to answer the *Why?* of the decennial summer pilgrimages. What, then, of the people themselves?

These Bavarians are peasants, a term which conveys a picture all its own, signifying a rustic— a tiller of the soil—one who lives close to Nature's heart. But when that heart means southern Bavaria, where Nature has evolved such charm and grandeur for her sons to dwell among, surely the student of the effect of environment upon the human spirit may look for, and reasonably expect to find, a unique type of peasant. Moreover, these peasants are said to belong to some of the oldest families of southern Europe, so that the cumulative effect of inspiring surroundings could be expected to be distinctly traceable in their development.

Their native dignity is remarkable—such as is found in almost any land, among those who live close to nature. Many a tourist must have been impressed with the dignified bearing and gracious manner of his host in this little village. In rough dress, suited to his daily toil as house-painter, or builder, or farmer, he must often have set an enviable example to his guest of high degree, hailing from one or another of the disintegrating civilizations of the outside world. Simple and unaffected, sincere and unafraid, he grasps one's hand with the grip of a friend. He may not be learned in the lore of the schools, but he knows the heart of man. He may not be versed in the new psychology or in the Freudian theories, but the " cardinal virtues " motivate his daily life. In all probability, he would marvel with the deep wonder of a child, at some of the deep-laid schemes and complex machinations of Wall Street and other bourses of the Western world, but his dealings are honest and his ideals high.

Yet it would be a grave error to suppose that these simple, unaffected people are weaklings, either mentally or physically. Their isolation and close fellowship with nature has resulted in a sturdy, rugged independence, which is evidenced in their well-knit figures, direct glance, and competent attitude, which seem to say: " What need is there of human aid? ' I will lift up mine eyes unto the hills, from whence cometh my help.' "

The location of their village, on the border line
lying between Bavaria and Austria, has brought to
them the tests of war and depredation, time and
again, and has fostered a high degree of courage
and patriotism. Their history holds vivid records
of former wars between the two countries, especially of the invasion of Napoleon, which caused
extreme suffering—almost starvation—in the village of Oberammergau. But with great courage
they kept their mountain village and their Play
intact.

Can it not be assumed that the attribute of
steady, dogged persistence, so marked in these
people, might have been fostered by their environment? What more likely? The enduring hills,
the constant forests, the ever-flowing river, have
all tended to deepen and strengthen the tenacious
purpose of these persistent peasants. To illustrate: In 1770, all religious plays were forbidden
by royal edict. In desperation, the villagers
pleaded with the civil and religious authorities for
permission to give their Passion Play. Permission
was not granted, however, and for the only time in
its history, the Play was omitted. But the matter
was not settled in the minds of the Oberammergauers, and they continued to present petition after
petition during the following ten years. Finally,
upon their preparing and presenting a new text,
privilege to resume the Play was granted by Karl
Theodore, Duke of Bavaria. But in 1800, another

edict forbade all such plays, with extreme penalty
for violation, and the special privilege granted
Oberammergau was withdrawn. The leaders of
the village fairly besieged the authorities at
Munich with petitions, and must have convinced
them of the virtue of their cause, for after tireless
effort they finally obtained the unusual grant to
henceforth present their Play each ten years as
they desired, with the reservation that each decennial presentation was to receive some measure of
sanction from the State. This, however, has come
to be regarded as a matter of form rather than a
permission, and the Oberammergau Passion Play
is looked upon by the authorities rather as a world
event than a local celebration.

Even in very early times, this village, with its
one consuming purpose, appeared to be different
from the neighbouring communities. It was especially favoured by the royal house of Bavaria, and
had certain rights and privileges similar to those
of the so-called " free cities " of Germany. And
similarly today. In the midst of a glorious region
of country dotted with picturesque and interesting
peasant settlements, Oberammergau is noticeably
of a different type, and village and villagers com-
bine to enable her to hold her own, as queen of the
Bavarian Highlands.

Again: shut in as these people are by the everlasting hills, they are a little world to themselves,
able to minister to their mutual material needs,

and relying upon one another for the meeting of
the varied demands of life—civic, social and religious. It naturally follows that they have
evolved a pure form of democratic government
which is headed by a Bürgermeister or mayor, who
is elected by the householders—nearly every citi-
zen is a householder and land owner—and there
is a village council, and the usual town officials.
The inhabitants number, all told, about two
thousand, having increased from sixteen hundred
in 1910.

That they are a law-abiding community in Oberammergau is indicated by the fact that there is
said to be no such institution in the town as a gaol,
and in normal times, very little poverty.

The majority of the villagers are tillers of the
soil, living quietly in their comfortable little
homes, and going out into their fields by day—
men, women, and children—leaving only the old
of both sexes behind, to do housework and, pre-
sumably, care for the babies. Besides tilling from
three to sixty acres of land apiece, they have all
the surrounding Alps for pasturage. The result is
six or seven hundred cows divided among the village families. As each cow wears a bell—each
horse and goat also—the music made by the itiner-
ating animals makes a lively sound, as they come
home at night to the milking-shed in the village.
They are then escorted through the one and only
real street to their various quarters, almost in the

very homes of their owners, or at least under
the same roof, a procedure eminently typical of
peasant life.

These people are progressive in many ways.
They have a fine water system, bringing the pure,
refreshing stream from mountain springs down
into each village home. They have a modern
method of disposing of sewage and use electricity
for light and transportation. They have turned
the Ammer from being an agent of destruction into
a beneficent and useful helper; for instead of con-
verting the valley into a stony marsh, by the volume of débris it brought down from the highlands
in flood time, it peacefully waters the fertile
meadows of the valley until they " blossom like
the rose."

The Oberammergau peasant is not raw, un-
refined, uneducated material. One may meet
here—it has been the case throughout their long
history—men of great ability as well as unusual
attainment. The only member of the delegation
of villagers which visited the United States in 1923,
who spoke English, was Anton Lang. Some of
the young people in the village speak it, and Mrs.
Lang speaks and writes it, having studied in
England before her marriage.

Frau Mathilda Lang, daughter of Jakob Rutz,
the former leader of the Chorus in which Mathilda
was the leading soprano, is a most capable and
efficient woman of rare business and executive

gifts. Besides rearing their interesting family of
six sons and daughters, she has continually stood
by her husband's side, inspiring him in his artistic
work, encouraging and sustaining him in that most
wearing experience of impersonating the *Christus*
of the Passion Play. She has also been a wonderful factor in the life of the village, and in admin-
istering help to the needy and afflicted.

Another export in a different line was Gregor
Breitsamter, one of the most interesting person-
alities in the village. He was a man of private
means, and had a fine villa with a most charming garden. His specialty was horticulture, of
which he had scientific knowledge. He played in
the important rôle of *Caiaphas* in 1910.

Herr Guido Lang, who died in 1924, must be included among the leading notables of the village.
Lang added to his home a museum which contains
the oldest Oberammergau manuscript in existence,
dating back to the year 1662. He also possessed a
remarkable collection of old Biblical dramas and
rosary plays, of which he was a connoisseur. In his
museum, too, are some fine specimens of religious
carvings, dating back to the fifteenth century.

There is much to be learned, it seems, even in
this peasant village shut up in the Bavarian hills,
and men of education and refinement are content
to live out their lives in its pleasant isolation, remote from the haunts of wealth and social prestige.

A number of the village leaders have had training in the schools of Munich, notably Ludwig Lang, the former Director of the Passion Play, who studied many years in the art schools of Munich, and was an authority on Italian art. Ludwig Lang possessed an executive ability which would have sufficed to manage a great railroad system or a large business corporation. His mastery of detail was remarkable—his artistic insight extraordinary. Small wonder that Oberammergau needed not to go beyond her own borders for leaders to stage her Play.

In times past such leaders were few, although the villagers hold to the belief that some one will always be raised up to carry on their stupendous undertaking. They mean to have it so, and began early to make it possible. A school of drawing was started in 1800, which has developed into a very modern and excellent School of Wood Carving. The prevailing idea in Oberammergau is, that every village child shall be given an opportunity to learn the village arts, and to be trained along the line in which he shows talent. It would appear as though a village of experts might result, provided the young people can be kept at home. So far, the incentive to roam appears to have been counteracted by the unusual interest taken in the life of the little Bavarian town. That one is a native of Oberammergau, and in line for a rôle in the Passion Play, is a fact that is regarded with justifiable pride.

It demands no lengthy observation of these people to convince one that, religiously, they are unusually developed. Partly, this is due to their uplifting surroundings—without doubt. Their beloved mountains inspiringly point upward, and their hearts respond. Then, too, their hands are largely busy with objects associated with religious worship, and, naturally, mind and thought direct the hands. It is partly due, however, to the fact of their proximity to the old monastery of Ettal, which has furnished them with leaders and teachers from the beginning of their history. Finally, lifelong familiarity with the subject of the Passion Play must and does have its formative effect.

Of course these villagers live in a land where the Roman Catholic Church holds sway, and here, as elsewhere in Papal strongholds, church and priest exercise supreme authority. Yet the Oberammergauer, although most devout, is singularly free from bigotry, and most tolerant of those holding other beliefs. Let no one suppose, however, that these villagers live in a state of religious fervour or are fanatical, in any respect. They love their Church and are attentive to its ritual. Early morning Mass is not neglected, and at the Angelus hour, the pealing of the chimes brings every one to a standstill, with raised cap, until the bells are silent. Yet they are anything but long-faced ascetics; they are human—very much so. " Say in your book, that we do not pose as saints," said one of the best known villagers, " but we are just like other people, no better, and I hope, no worse."

But whether better or worse, one realizes that, in this old-world village, he may come upon a combination that is certainly unique. He will discover a remarkable type of peasant—independent, patriotic, self-respecting, democratic, in many cases highly cultivated, and, religiously, unusually developed. It is a phenomenon worth the study of social experts. Even to the casual summer tourist, driving through the picturesque highlands of the Tyrolese Alps, this particular village stands out as being different, and the villagers as possessing peculiar charm.

But is this all? Does this differing element explain the great decennial influx of visitors? Does *this* answer the *Why?*

V

THE PEOPLE: AT WORK AND PLAY

TO attain a better understanding of the character of this unique people, one turns to another sidelight in their history. In mediæval times, Oberammergau lay on the direct line of travel from Italy to the cities of Northern Germany. Great merchant-caravans made their way up through the mountain passes to the plains beyond, and, quite often, needed assistance of the villagers in transporting their precious cargoes. If they arrived in Oberammergau on Saturday, it was customary to entertain them over Sunday, and to assist them on their journey the following day.

This brought the villagers into contact with foreign people and foreign customs, both in a business and social way. It may account, in part, for the ease with which the Oberammergauer adapts himself to strangers. Furthermore, as was only natural, a certain amount of mutual attraction existed between German maid and Italian youth, and quite a number of the village names indicate that frequent intermarriages took place. In course of time, Italian blood was flowing in

the veins of these Bavarian mountaineers, and
Italian characteristics blended with the German.
Thus we trace, in part at least, the origin of the
villagers' artistic genius. The native instinct has
been nurtured by beautiful natural environment,
and by daily employment of a refining and uplifting character. As might have been expected, generation after generation of such development has
resulted in an art-loving and art-producing people
of outstanding note.

A Drawing School was established in the village
over a hundred years ago, and wood-carving introduced in very early times. Nobody knows just
when or how, but it is generally attributed to the
monks of the monastery of Ettal. Nearly four
hundred years ago a traveller, writing a history of
Ettal, referred to the villagers of Oberammergau
as being carvers of wonderful figures from wood,
and able to fashion a crucifix out of a nutshell!

In the museum of Guido Lang, whose great-
grandfather established the first store for the sale
of the village wares, there are religious carvings
which date back to the fifteenth century. Lang
also has a collection of curious figures, not more
than two or three inches high, some of which are
jointed and made to sit in tiny carriages drawn
by perfect little horses, all carved and painted in
the character of court personages of two centuries ago.

Another group of carvings which is quite

famous is the Nativity group, carved about a
century ago. These carvings were originally kept
in the church, and shown at Christmas time.
There are a hundred carved, movable figures, sixteen inches high, and one hundred and twenty
animals, represented as being on their way to the
manger and the Christ Child. This set is on exhibition in the house of the sculptor Johann Georg
Lang, and attracts much attention.

The village wood-carving industry has had its
ups and downs. Originally, the carvings were
peddled from place to place. Then came a period
of prosperity, when some of the families of Oberammergau owned ships which sailed the North,
the Baltic, and even the Black Sea, and when the
village wares were carried into Spain, France,
Italy, Holland, and Russia. Later, there were
periods of depression, but since about 1850, a
steadily increasing business has been maintained,
and the carvings are now sold all over Europe.
More recently, a market has been established in
both North and South America.

About two hundred of the villagers earn their
living by wood carving, and it should be noted
that their work is largely of a religious character
—crucifixes, rosaries, altars, decorative figures,
large and small, for ecclesiastical uses. There are
also toys of all descriptions; and set pieces of
which " The Last Supper " is a favourite subject. Peter Rendl's " Last Supper," an exquis-

itely done plaque, has acquired a wide reputation, and is the choice possession of many visitors to Oberammergau.

The Drawing School which was established about 1800, has developed into the very excellent School for Wood Carving, of which mention already has been made. The first building was erected in 1888, but was soon outgrown. In 1909, with funds at least partially earned by the Passion Play, and augmented by a grant from the Bavarian Landtag and other contributions, the sum of one hundred and seven thousand marks was secured, and the present modern and adequate building erected, and trained teachers placed in charge.

Just as the actors in the Passion Play have tended to hold on to the same rôle as long as possible, so the village artists have held to their specialties, such as Rendl with his "Last Supper," some with their crucifixes, and others with the figure of Christ. But the future carvers are being given scientific training with a knowledge of drawing as a foundation; and a wider variety of subjects and richness of treatment is already evidenced.

A notable example of development is found in the very intricate, delicate, ornamental and allegorical carvings, done by Alois Lang for the magnificent organ, in the chancel of the new chapel of the University of Chicago. It is a remarkable

VILLAGERS ON THEIR WAY HOME FROM CHURCH

artistic achievement—one destined to endure. It
is interesting to contrast this modern example with
the carvings of earlier days—the Nativity group,
for example. Of course, the subject is entirely
different; but is it not also true that there is less
skill and more art in the organ carvings? The
work of these mountaineer wood-carvers has been
criticized in this respect,—that their skill has out-
run their art, especially since the medium they
use is wood, which demands a broader stroke, a
less finished treatment. It has been said in criticism that they might as well work in ivory, and
possibly, the chapel carvings justify this criticism to a certain extent. There is inspiring freedom of design and workmanship, combined with
a sublime effect. Yet the spirit is the same as
that which animates the work of older carvers,
away in the isolated village in the hills of Bavaria.

An artistic instinct seems to pervade the very
atmosphere of this Bavarian village. It is seen,
also, in the faces of the villagers, which are not
stolid and expressionless, but sensitive and alert.
One writer has noted the fine, well-formed hands
of the artists of Oberammergau.

There are incidents of the innate love of beauty
to be met with, even in unexpected quarters.
Mrs. Louise Parks-Richards writes of a butcher's
boy who came from the slaughter-house to point
out to her a picturesque view of the Ammer,
where she might use her camera to good effect.

Her stage-driver exclaimed with delight over a sketch she showed him, and commented on it with the discrimination of a real artist. "It was only an Oberammergauer mountain driver," adds Mrs. Richards, "who was a hangman in the Passion Play; but he had the heart of an artist, and its chords were responsive to the lightest touch." King Ludwig must have felt this unusual and peculiar village atmosphere, when he dedicated his marble group to "the art-loving Oberammergauers."

Where else in the world would it be possible to look into a village home on a winter evening, and see a whole family—father, mother and four children—seated about a table intent on their carving, each doing what he or she could do best, with even the grandmother, who had begun to carve when she was twelve, producing the crucifix she had carved? Yet this was a picture actually to be seen in the home of Andreas Lang, the *Peter* of the Passion Play, and one of the most skilled of the village wood-carvers.

Mrs. Richards tells us that this man suggested her giving him a subject for a carving he had never attempted, and proposed to execute it in half an hour! She suggested David, the shepherd boy, whom his son had been representing in one of the village plays. Lang sawed off a section of the limb of a pear-tree, and started to cut and chisel seemingly at random. Soon, however, the outline of a figure began to appear, and in just thirty minutes time he handed Mrs. Richards a beautiful sketch of the shepherd boy, David, with his harp.

It must not be supposed that wood carving is the only art practiced in the village. There are sculptors of real merit and painters in oil and water colour. There is weaving of textiles, and fine needlework, reminiscent of olden days, is undertaken. There is also at least one expert in the making of marionettes; and workers in metal show candlesticks, boxes and ornamental figures of various descriptions.

There are those, too (of whom Johann Zwinck is perhaps best known), who decorate in appropriate colour the carved figures and other productions of their brother artists.

But, next to carving, the most important art in the village is ceramics. Anton Lang is the leading potter, and is ably assisted by his son, Karl, now a young man of real artistic talent. They have made a scientific study of this interesting branch of art, and show a wide variety of productions—from porcelain stoves and ornamental tile to all kinds of dishes, jars, bowls and vases of delicate workmanship and exquisite colouring. Karl has been especially interested in experimenting in new processes of glazing, and both father and son are experts in their chosen line.

A village of peasant farmers, say you? But it is also a village of artists! And is this all? Has the *Why?* been answered? No; in order to understand fully the genius of this peculiar people, it is necessary to point out another phase of their artistic natures, and to turn back another page of their history.

Dramatic instinct is natural to human kind. Where is the child who does not possess it? To " pretend "—to act a part—is it not as natural, as spontaneous in him as to run and jump? So, also, in the childhood of the race, we expect and are able to find a fondness for play-acting. The so-called " folk-drama " is found among all races, and nowhere, since the days of ancient Greece, has drama acquired such a hold upon a people as in Bavaria. From the earliest times down to the present, the drama has been considered an essential part of the education of the people. Munich is called "Athens upon the Isar," and her students, today, are among the most faithful attendants at the Hof Theatre.

In the rural districts, also, there is no place so secluded or remote as to remain undiscovered by troupes of wandering actors, or that has not its own little dramas, based upon religious or local history. In the Middle Ages, the monks, with little in the way of recreation, were accustomed to write and present religious plays on the various church holidays. They were given in the church

building or, preferably, the churchyard. The
subjects were usually Biblical, although sometimes old Greek plays were adapted. The Bavarian people, also, with musical as well as histrionic
ability, sometimes produced musical dramas.

There is historical evidence that, as early as
the fifth century, Biblical plays were presented
in England. But the Anglo-Saxon outgrew this
form of art, while among some of the German
peoples it persisted. Especially among the peasants of the mountainous districts, with their
artistic natures and deep religious feeling, it was
only natural that the religious drama should maintain its hold.

Of all religious subjects, the Passion of our
Lord appears to have been the favourite, because
of its dramatic possibilities. Within the last hundred years Passion Plays have been presented in
as many as sixty different Bavarian villages, but
it is in Oberammergau *alone* that *the* Passion Play
is given today. In no other place *could* it be
given. " In any other place," declares Stoddard,
the travel lecturer, " the Passion Play would be
offensive."

Every now and then, one hears of sporadic
Passion Plays being produced in various old-
world towns; even in America, attempts are sometimes made to present so-called Passion Plays.
Sooner or later, however, they are heard of no
more, while the appeal of the Oberammergau

Play becomes more and more compelling, with the passing years. Evidently the world desires to help Oberammergau retain her play and keep her vow, for in the Bavarian village the tradition persists that the Play is the fulfilment of a religious vow.

The story is told in an old chronicle, which is preserved in the village archives. According to this chronicle, a terrible pestilence visited Germany in the year 1633, one of the results of the Thirty Years War. Whole villages were wiped out, but Oberammergau maintained a strict quarantine, and, for a time, escaped disaster. Unfortunately, a poor fellow named Caspar Shüsler—the name has been carefully preserved in the chronicle—who was working in a neighbouring town, desired to spend Sunday with his family, broke through the quarantine, and carried death and destruction with him. In thirty-three days, nearly a hundred of the villagers had perished. In their despair, the people betook themselves to their one resource—God. Their extremity was great, but their faith greater, and God able to save! So the villagers pledged themselves to a certain course—for all time to periodically render their Passion Play, in return for their deliverance. The compact was made, and—sceptical criticism to the contrary, notwithstanding—the records state that, from that hour, the plague was stayed. The following year, the Play was given in fulfilment

of the vow, and from that time until the present—
nearly three hundred years—and in spite of many
obstacles, the vow has been kept.

After 1674, the Play was put on an even decennial basis, and from 1680 to the present time,
it has been omitted but once—in 1770—when all
plays were prohibited by a royal edict (see page
39). Repeated importunity gained permission to
resume it in 1780, and since that date, each tenth
year has witnessed its performance, except when
the ruthless hand of war has laid hands upon the
performers, and necessitated its postponement.
This happened in 1870, when it was delayed one
year by the Franco-Prussian struggle. Again, as
1920 drew near, the little community, crippled
and impoverished by the World War, sadly relinquished its plans for the Play. By 1922, however, it had rallied its forces, made the necessary
preparations and, in spite of almost insuperable
obstacles, most magnificently fulfilled its vow.

Thus is discovered an unique combination—the
peasant *artists* of Oberammergau are *actors* as
well! When asked what, of all things, he would
prefer to do, one of the leading wood-carvers of
the village, who had supported as many as seventy different rôles, replied: " If I had everything
the world could give I should still be a wood-
carver and find my greatest happiness here at my
carving-bench. The next best thing I love, is to
act in a play."

What a picture it is—a whole village, young and old, at play together! Andreas Lang acting David the king, in the same play with his son as David the shepherd boy! Parents and children, babies and their grandsires, sharing their interests and good times as a great joyous family! Naturally, there could be no need for such an institution as a *gaol*, in a village such as Oberammergau!

Three centuries of play-acting has rendered the histrionic ability inborn in these people. It is said that the babies pose naturally, just as soon as they can stand, and that the children in the streets are heard rehearsing the parts their fathers are acting!

A word should be appended concerning the children of Oberammergau. Such interesting youngsters, both boys and girls, with long, waving locks and graceful poses. Even babes in arms are carried in the tableaux of the Passion Play, and the self-control and rigidity of little tots, three or four years old, in the postures they are expected to hold, is amazing. They trot on and off the stage, with their little bare brown feet, with the self-possession of experienced actors.

Play-acting is the chief amusement of all the children, large and small, and they know their lines. As soon as a child learns to talk, he begins rehearsing parts of some rôle in a play, and as he grows old enough, he takes his part in the plays with his elders. They become very familiar with

Scripture, through the Biblical plays. Of course, David and Goliath is a favourite subject. But one little group was discovered, each with a shepherd's crook, and each in the rôle of a disciple, going up to Jerusalem. Even " The Last Supper " appeals to their desire for action. Thus they reflect the life of their elders, who are continually giving plays, both secular and religious, for recreation and to try out their abilities, with the Passion Play as the aim and crowning achievement of the village life.

Here, then, is the answer to the *Why?* of the decennial pilgrimages to the little village in the Bavarian Highlands. What is the quest—a shrine? Not in the accepted sense of that term. A miracle? a wonder surely! *A Play!* A Play given by simple mountaineers—amateurs—turning aside from their regular trades and vocations for the moment; a Play given in the open air, as nearly as may be, and lasting the whole day long.

These Oberammergau wood-carvers, and farmers, and painters and potters, in their native town, on a homemade stage, in garments designed and made in their midst, in their natural voices and with no artificial make-up, speaking and singing lines and music composed by their own leaders and teachers, have received, and are receiving, the homage of the greatest singers, the most noted actors, the most thoughtful students of the drama in all the world. Truly, " the Play's the thing! "

PART TWO

THE PLAY AND THE PLAYERS

VI

THE PLAY: ITS ORIGIN AND HISTORY

WHILE the origin of drama must be sought for in the inmost nature of human kind, yet external conditions have largely determined its form in any stated period. Thus, in the early Middle Ages, when there was little learning, and what there was, largely the possession of priests and monks, a favourite way to disseminate knowledge and to teach moral lessons was by symbol and action. This method also afforded recreation and satisfied the artistic instinct both of actor and spectator. Hence the mystery and miracle plays of the Middle Ages in England, dramatizing Bible stories and legends; later, came the morality plays, in which vices and virtues were personified and presented as pursuing their varied activities and conflicts.

In Germany, the folk drama has persisted, with variations, since the ninth century. Usually, Bible subjects were presented, or themes growing out of old pagan beliefs and customs. Sometimes, bits of local history were utilized, to tickle the primitive ear, much as the local allusions in a modern comedy amuse audiences of today.

Christmas plays were popular, of course; then came great spectacular festival plays, requiring a whole village as stage and all its villagers as actors. Such a play, preserved in *Meister Trunk*, is still given in the mediæval town of Rothenberg.

Religious plays were the natural outlet of the artistic bent of the children of nature dwelling in the mountain villages of Europe, especially in Bavaria. It has been commonly observed, that religion and art are closely akin, especially among those who live near to the soil. To such people natural phenomena constitute an expression of spiritual forces, inseparably linked with the ideal and beautiful. And the outward expression of the ideal and beautiful spells art—the artistic work of their hands, their music, their drama. The Crusades aroused the religious fervour of Europe in the eleventh century, and stimulated the production of religious plays. Of course, the soul-stirring story of the Lord's Passion appealed to the people in a degree not attained by any other subject, and was widely presented.

As was to be expected, with human nature what it was (and still is), objectionable features began to creep into these religious plays. The Passion Play was no exception. A bit of comedy could not be resisted, so Satan was represented as an ass, and figured ludicrously in many a scene. Judas, also, was caricatured unmercifully, which,

at various times, induced the ban of the civil and
religious authorities.

There is no account of the Passion Play having
been given in Oberammergau until undertaken by
the villagers in 1634, as the solemn performance
of their sacred religious vow, to which reference
has already been had. From that time on, its
history is clearly defined. That it has always
been different from the Passion Plays given in
many other places, is evidenced by the fact that,
when prohibited by the authorities elsewhere, it
was permitted in Oberammergau. Evidence of
the unusual confidence felt in the performers of
this village is shown by the fact of permanent permission to produce the Play, being finally bestowed
upon them in the year 1800.

The oldest text of the Passion Play now extant,
dates back to 1662, and the manuscript is exhibited by the oldest business firm in Oberammergau, Georg Lang, sel. Erben. It is stated by
students that this text is composed from two still
older—one used in Augsburg in the fifteenth century; the other, the work of the Meistersinger,
Sebastian Wild, and written about the middle of
the sixteenth century. The latter text, bearing
some traces of burlesque, was replaced by a revision after 1740, but without much improvement
being made. In 1780, still another revision was
made by one of the Paters of Ettal, at the request
of the villagers. The present text was written in

1810-15 by Pater Ottmar Weiss, and finally revised, improved and beautified by the "good angel" of the village, the beloved Father Daisenberger. The songs are said to be as written, in 1810, almost word for word; but the text of the Play proper, has been virtually transformed.

The text of the Play simply records the events in the last week of the earthly life of Jesus Christ, commencing with the triumphal entry into Jerusalem. The story adheres closely to the New Testament account. The words spoken by the *Christus* are largely the Biblically recorded words. The other lines are dignified, refined and, at times, strikingly Scriptural. Of course, it is in German, of a pure, strong and vigorous type, and bears about the same relation to the language of the people, as the King James Version of the Bible bears to the spoken English of today.

The translation of the text which those who do not understand German must follow, is a quite literal one, and in the songs and prologues somewhat disappointing; in the dialogue, however, it is very satisfactory. Father Daisenberger made a second revision of the text in 1880, doing it over into blank verse. This was submitted to the council, but, fortunately (as it seems today), they did not dare to attempt to change the lines so radically. The old text was of the warp and woof of the very lives of many of the villagers, not only of the leading actors but of many of

JOSEF MEYER, A SCULPTOR, WHO PLAYS THE PART OF A RABBI, AT HIS WORK

the understudies, and it seemed hazardous to trust the memories of middle-aged men with the new lines.

In 1883, some scholars in Munich desired to inject some modern ideas into the text, but the people of Oberammergau objected. For while minor alterations are sometimes made—in 1922, the Play was somewhat shortened—it was deemed unwise to make any radical change in language and sentiment which are spoken as from the very hearts of the people.

Bavaria is a land of music, and the musical drama flourishes there. Munich has been called the " Mecca of song." This is largely due to the efforts and influence of that unfortunate monarch, Ludwig II., and his enthusiastic sponsoring of the Wagnerian compositions. Unrivalled opportunities are offered for musical students as well as for travellers by the wonderful musical festivals held in Munich, Bayreuth, Nuremberg and Salzburg. It was to be expected, therefore, that there would be music in Oberammergau.

Since music contributes so largely to its effect, the Passion Play, in a sense, is a musical drama. It is difficult to comment upon the music, and there is great difference of opinion about it. It is called " superlatively bad " by one critic, and held to contain " a great number of sublime parts " by another. To be sure, the Play is not given for the sake of the music, the music being introduced for the sake of the Play. Nevertheless, one can hardly deny, that the best and most appropriate music possible would enhance the general effect of the Play. But critics should take into account the specific purpose of the music— that of being a background for the lines and the action. It is entirely subsidiary to the text, and, in that respect, answers its purpose well. It does not monopolize the spectator's attention, unless, possibly, that of the super-sensitive musical critic, and a good deal of it is in the minor and, in the main, low-pitched.

The score was composed by a native of Oberammergau, Rochus Dedler, the village schoolmaster, a talented musician and a master of instrumentation. It is music adapted to an older day and meant to be given a quite simple rendition. It was first written in 1810, but the score was destroyed by fire, whereupon Dedler composed new music for the play of 1820. Various attempts have been made to improve it, but these have only succeeded in marring it. Now, it has been decided to leave the score pretty much as it was originally written. It has never been published, except in excerpts, accompanied by an introduction by the teacher, Ludwig Wittman, the musical director of the orchestra and chorus.

An orchestra of forty pieces, placed in a recess and hidden from the audience, is used in the Passion Play. There is also a chorus of forty singers, intended to represent a group of guardian angels, which takes the place of the chorus in the old Greek plays, advancing with a prologuist to the front of the stage before the commencement of each act, to explain to the audience the character of what is to follow.

The Prologuist has an important rôle. He introduces the tableaux and chorus, and comments upon the subject of the tableau about to be shown, linking it up with the specific event in the life of Christ it is intended to prefigure. Solos are occasionally introduced by the choragus—the leader of the chorus—or some other leading voice, and artistic musical effects are produced by a quartette of women's voices, by invisible singers and in other simple ways.

But, in the main, the procedure is very simple. For instance: the overture finished, the chorus advances, garbed in graceful draperies of rich, harmonious colouring. The singers enter from the wings in two divisions, one at either end of the stage. They advance slowly and take their places at the front of the proscenium. The choragus steps forward and sings a welcome. Next, a spectacular tableau assembles in the pavilion in the centre of the stage. This tableau, the chorus accompanies with song. At this point the Prologuist appears, and recites his explanation of the tableau and its application to the immediately approaching experience of the Christ. The

act, with its various scenes, is then given. This
is the order followed at the beginning of the
Play, but the order, in general, is:—prologue,
tableau, chorus, and the next act in proper
sequence.

The tableaux form a most important feature of
the whole, and the idea, to whomsoever the credit
may belong, is a most happy one. Each act is
preceded by one or two remarkable ensembles,
some of them including hundreds of persons, men,
women and children. The ensemble reflects the
genius of a group-painter of the highest artistic
skill, as does the costuming and colouring. There
is no artificial lighting, be it remembered, so that
the poses and expressions are not synthetically
enhanced in any way; yet the effects produced are
truly marvellous.

As already stated, these tableaux illustrate the
subject of the act which immediately follows. For
example: the Crucifixion is preceded by two tableaux: " Isaac Bearing the Wood for the Sacrifice," and " Moses Lifting Up the Serpent in the
Wilderness." Of course, considerable time is consumed by these prologue-tableau-chorus interludes,
and the critic who proposes the shortening of the
Play suggests their omission. They occupy, perhaps, about half the time covered by the Play as
a whole.

But if one try to imagine the Play being rendered without the interludes, the conclusion will

at once be reached that they are needed. They answer a double purpose. Not only do they prefigure artistically the event they are intended to introduce, but they serve to relieve the tension of the audience. To watch this tragic story unfolded in its entirety, and without relaxation, would be well-nigh unendurable.

The Passion Play is presented in three parts, eighteen acts and twenty-four tableaux. It is planned to begin at eight o'clock in the morning and to last until six in the evening, with a two-hour intermission in the middle of the day. Formerly, it was given entirely in the open air, just outside the churchyard, the walls of which served to hold the rough boards of the stage. Such was the scene of the Play, the mountains the background, the blue sky or clouded heavens the canopy, a grassy plot the auditorium; but there was no scenery, no seat, no text-book. As time passed, the Play was put more and more under cover, until today it is housed in the great theatre, built in 1900, improved in 1910, enlarged somewhat in 1922, and recently rebuilt so as to accommodate five thousand people.

The Passion Play season begins about the middle of May, and lasts sixteen weeks—until the last of September. Thirty-two presentations are announced, with the understanding that more will be given if there be demand for them. In 1922, there *was* such a demand, and sixty-six presentations

were given, and multitudes of people crowded the
theatre, to be held spellbound by the tragic fascina-
tion of the " old, old Story," portrayed before their
very eyes.

Illustrious spectators, from every part of the
world, have journeyed to Oberammergau, and
joined the great audience gathered in the Passion
Play theatre.   Among them have been the five
kings of Bavaria, Queen Isabella of Spain, the
German Emperor Friedrich Wilhelm when Crown
Prince of Prussia, King Edward VII. as Prince of
Wales, Richard Wagner, Adelina Patti, and many
of the famous singers and actors of the world.
At the opening of the season, in 1922, fully half
of those present were Americans, the English
coming next, with Russians, Dutch and Germans
making up the assemblage.

But the performance of the Play which is always
given just before the regular season begins, appeals strongly to one's imagination.   For on that
occasion the Oberammergau players present their
Play to their peasant neighbours, from all the
country round about.   It is *their* day, and it has
been computed that as many as eight thousand
have flocked to the village, eager and expectant,
and have crowded the theatre to witness the great
Play, feeling, no doubt, a proprietary interest in
the production.   Surely this audience must be
regarded as being more sympathetic and understanding than any other, and as a demonstration

of friendliness and brotherhood, is a most striking occasion.

The great cosmopolitan audiences which as-ocmble during the summer months have moved Anton Lang to express the hope that " the Passion Play will constitute a basis for a more friendly intercourse between nation and nation and result in a better international understanding." In that hope, all right-thinking people, the world over, must surely desire to join.

VII

THE PLAY: ITS INSPIRATION AND SPIRIT

A S we have already noted, the Passion Play is presented at Oberammergau every ten years. But the interest evinced in this unique expression of religious art is perennial and constant.

As to its subject—the last week in the earthly life of Our Lord—there is, at first, a thought that the idea of theatrically staging the sad events of Holy Week, may appear to be presumptuous, almost sacrilegious, and many shrink from witnessing a dramatization of the physical suffering of Jesus. Yet, after all, what subject can be conceived of, which appeals so strongly to the universal mind and heart? What other story is there in history or fiction, which combines so many elements of commonly shared interest, as this story of the " human side of the martyrdom of Jesus "? As Hermine Diemer says in her soul-stirring description of The Scourging and Crown of Thorns scene: " It is all so cruelly yet quietly carried out, that it cuts into our very souls without, at the same time, offending our æsthetic feelings." And what other story can be

recalled, which exhibits so many authentic phases
of human nature—envy, cowardice, treachery:
patience, loyalty, devotion and forgiveness, human
and divine?

The effort to make this story visible to the eyes
of mankind, was the beginning and inspiration of
mediæval art. It has been carved in marble,
painted upon canvas, wrought in crystal. It has
been made the subject of unnumbered volumes,
and, quite naturally, has appealed strongly to the
dramatic instinct—with the result that, in Oberammergau at least, it is portrayed in *life*, by devout
men and women. And, after all, does not the
character of the actors and their motives, deter-
mine the effect of a production of such a nature?
The underlying motive of the presentation is best
expressed in a quotation from the address of the
good priest Daisenberger, delivered to his flock,
before the Passion Play season of 1870:

" If we work together in holy zeal worthily to represent these great mysteries," he said, " then we may
expect that with God's grace, great blessings may en-
sue. Many pious Christians, touched with emotion by
the representations of the Saviour's death, will return
home edified and strengthened in their faith and love.
Many of the lukewarm and frivolous, unable to throw
off the solemn impressions they have received, will, in
the future, show that the seeds of a more Christian life
were sown here. And it may be that the sight of the
Redeemer's great love for mankind may draw tears
from the eyes of sinners, and these tears, aided by

God's good Spirit, may be the way by which the good
Shepherd seeks and finds His lost sheep."

Not every Oberammergauer, perhaps, looks upon
the Passion Play with the same purity of motive
as did Father Daisenberger; but it is certain that
the general attitude of the performers and of the
villagers as a whole, is, that the Play is the solemn
fulfilment of a sacred vow, and their own peculiar
contribution to the world's religious art.

" It is not only the greatest honour of my life
to represent the character of Jesus," said Josef
Mayr, the *Christus* of 1870–'80–'90, " but it is
for me, also, the most solemn of religious duties."

Each day's performance is preceded by an early
morning service in the village church, and behind
the curtain on the stage just before the orchestra
begins the overture, the entire company of performers may be found grouped about their director, repeating their Pater Noster in unison.

The attitude of the players toward their Play
may find fitting illustration in the final acts of the
season, as described by eye-witnesses—particularly
Mrs. Louise Parks-Richards, who has lived in the
village and speaks with authority.

The actors are greatly agitated as the climax
of their summer effort approaches, and their
pent-up feelings move them to tears as they grasp
each others' hands after the closing tableaux and
the last strain of the orchestra finale is heard.

The *Christus* makes his way to his study. "Don't turn on the light," he says. His little daughter climbs into his lap, troubled by her father's pensive mien. Yet, must it not always be so—that any one who essays to enter, deeply and intimately, into the experiences of the Man of Sorrows, must needs be sad, as he realizes how slowly this troubled world is responding to the appeal of redeeming love? Yet Lang has kept his faith and hopes that the Play "may aid in forgetting the Hymn of Hate, and may be a real feast of reconciliation."

In the evening the *Christus* meets the disciples for a final supper. The women of the Play also meet together, and the scribes and Pharisees gather to say farewell. The next morning a thanksgiving service is held in the church, the whole village assembling to render thanks for the successful completion of their great undertaking. The entire orchestra is present, together with the full chorus, who render one of the compositions of Dedler, the composer of the Passion Play music. After the service, the congregation pass out into the churchyard, and march before the laurel-crowned bust of their beloved priest, Daisenberger, in remembrance of his great service to people and Play. Adjournment to the theatre, for a special farewell ceremony, is then made. There are but a handful in the great auditorium, which has been housing its thousands all summer.

The Bürgermeister takes his place on the open
proscenium, with the village priest by his side. On
his right is grouped the orchestra, on his left, the
members of the local council.

The Bürgermeister speaks feelingly of the summer's work, and of the evident approval of heaven
vouchsafed them in the fulfilment of their vow.
"And now, my dear Oberammergauers," he says in
conclusion, " as we return to our several occupations, let us seek to live in peace, love and con-
cord." The people rise and join in silent prayer,
as the orchestra plays a final choral.

The following morning, the concluding act of
the season is performed. Every man, woman and
child who can walk, is on the road to Ettal before
sunrise. Upon arrival at the monastery, a morning Mass is celebrated with stately music, and
breakfast served in the refectory. The return
march is then begun, and ends at the village
church, whence, after a short prayer, the company
is dispersed. The Play is a thing of the past;
and the actors are simply Rendl and Mayr and
Lang and the rest, ordinary villagers for the coming decade instead of disciples, and priests, and
scribes and Pharisees.

Imagine a cast of actors in a modern drama, or
a group of operatic stars, signalizing the close of
their season in any such long-drawn-out and
serious manner! Yet the idea that this is a village of religious enthusiasts and fanatics is to be

rigidly guarded against. These people are very
human; they are, moreover, of the Teutonic type,
calm, content with their achievement, fixed in
ideas and observances, more modest in their re-
quirements, more practical in their attitude than
their high-strung, sentimental, idealistic Anglo-
Saxon brethren. The love of acting, too, inborn
and nurtured for three centuries, must be taken
into account, together with their religious motives, in attempting any adequate understanding
of their mental relation toward their momentous
undertaking. For the Passion Play is the one
great decennial event in the personal life of each
one of these villagers, just as it is in the history
of the village itself.

Probably the one man who, more than any
other, is responsible for the community's loyalty
to its tradition, is the priest, Joseph Alois Daisenberger. Born near Oberammergau and educated
at the monastery of Ettal, he was, in truth, a
native product of those gracious, uplifting, stimu-
lating Bavarian hills. He became the village
priest in 1845, and from that time until his death
was, in reality, as well as name, a true Father to
the village—equally beloved and revered. A man
of unusual intellect, Daisenberger was extraordi-
narily broad-minded in ideas, precepts and actions.
He held his flock to strict obedience in the observance of their religious duties, yet he taught,
and *lived*, true Christian brotherhood and charity.

He was companion and friend as well as priest, and entered into the daily life of his flock, even writing secular plays for them, and translating *Antigone* from the Greek in order that they might test their powers in classical drama. But the Passion Play was his great life-work, and he studied so assiduously to improve it, that it is to him that we owe its present form. With childlike persistence, he laboured to do this one thing, and he has made of the Play a living force.

Yet a modern critic, writing after the Play of 1922, claimed that Daisenberger spoiled the Passion Play. True, if it *be* spoiled, the good priest spoiled it! But what does this critic advise? To shorten it by one half; to cut out the interludes; to get a great actor to train the players, and an expert to handle the crowds. He also scores the music and sarcastically condemns the scenery, which is introduced for the tableaux and interior scenes. He commends the costumes and the splendid colour scheme; he admits there are moments when one realizes what possibilities of beauty and spiritual significance the Play contains. Nevertheless, he would speed it up, and have it given at night!

But what, then, would the Play have become? Could Bethany be reproduced in modern dress? Would one wish to behold Calvary presented according to the methods of present-day secular drama? The very question answers itself. The thing would be a travesty—not a unique, old-world, traditional production, drawn from the very hearts of its actors and embodying their highest spiritual ideals. No; Father Daisenberger did *not* spoil the Passion Play—that would be the testimony of the vast majority of those who have breathlessly watched its progress from morn until eve; who have gone away refreshed of soul and quickened in holy purpose. The good priest says that he did his work simply " for the love of the Redeemer, and for the edification of the Christian world," and that work is truly Christian. Catholic doctrine is not obtruded, while the idea of the brotherhood of man is held consistently in view.

It is a notable and a significant fact that, in Bavaria, a country almost mediæval in impression, and Catholic to the core, in a great theatre with an audience of four thousand persons of all sorts and conditions, from all parts of the world, of all shades of belief and unbelief, such is the atmosphere produced as the Play proceeds that there seems to be neither Catholic nor Protestant, neither sect nor creed. The Church of God appears to be once more united, or in view of what is going on before the eye, it was never divided— " One is your Master, even Christ, and all ye are brethren."

So free from bigotry was the good priest, and so worthily do his pupils enter into his spirit!

A bronze bust was erected in his honour in the village churchyard. It is inscribed simply: "His works do follow him," as in very truth they do, for his abiding monument is the Oberammergau Passion Play.

JESUS AND HIS DISCIPLES ON THE WAY TO BETHANY

VIII

THE PLAY: PREPARATIONS AND RESULTS

THE preparations for the Passion Play require at least a year. Long before that, however, plans are taking shape in the minds of the leaders. Possible candidates for the important rôles are being considered, and ways and means for financing the project definitely discussed.

What an exciting experience it must be for the promising young Oberammergauer who has been testing his ability in the plays of everyday life to note that the eyes of the community are upon him; to learn that his name is being whispered about from lip to lip; that, maybe, the rôle of *John the Beloved* will fall to his lot! Or, possibly, it is the part of *Mary the Mother* that is in store for the young woman who has found herself developing in ability and growing in grace! Like any other coveted prizes, these Passion Play rôles are watched and worked for with earnest zeal. " It took me just fifty-three years to get my *Herod*," says Rochus Lang. To the Oberammergauer the greatest honour that can be achieved is to sustain one of the important rôles in the Passion Play.

All preparations for the Passion Play are in the hands of a special committee, consisting of the fourteen members of the town council, the parish priest as an honourary member, and six persons elected for the purpose by the villagers. Of this committee, the Bürgermeister is chairman. The specially appointed body appoints all sub-committees, selects the members of the chorus, and elects the principal actors by secret ballot. The actors must all be natives of Oberammergau. Any newcomers in the village must feel decidedly left out of it, as did the little girl, who said with tearful voice: " I am not an Oberammergauer, and so I can't be in the Play. But I *should* like to have a part with the rest of the children."

The director discusses each rôle in detail and explains the qualifications necessary to its proper maintenance, after which nominations are made by secret ballot. After two weeks of deliberation, the committee, in a body, proceeds to the church for a religious service, at which the final vote is taken, each member dropping a white or black ball into an urn, as the candidates' names are presented. Thus are the principal actors elected; and for a hundred years it has been the custom to make their names public on the fifth day of December preceding the season of the Play.

Meanwhile, the whole village is in a state of

suspense and excitement, for everybody is interested and concerned. Each male inhabitant has a part assigned, if only as an usher or fireman in the wings. All the young people are included and about two hundred children. Only the married women, and any newcomers to the village, are left out. To the former falls the task of taking care of the horde of hungry tourists which is to descend upon the village. "The provident providers of provender," these hard-working *hausfrauen* have been called. And right adequately have they lived up to the name.

Understudies are provided, and indeed the whole village becomes so familiar with the various rôles that there is said to be no difficulty in providing substitutes, in case of sickness or accident.

The rôles distributed, each actor must agree, in solemn contract, that he will perform his task to the best of his ability. Any conduct on his part inimical to the Play or the community mulcts him in a fine, or the losing of his appointed part. No amusements or gaieties are permitted during Passion year; the usual carnival season, just before Lent, is given up; even those who desire to be married according to the hilarious Bavarian customs, must postpone the wedding until after the Passion season is over. Rehearsals take place almost nightly for five months, the performers actually *living* their rôles, even being called and referred to by the names they assume in the Play.

In 1922, there were about eight hundred performers, and of these about one hundred had speaking parts. The majority of the actors are wood-carvers by trade; but there are also farmers, painters, a baker, a shoemaker, a road-mender, a canal-tender. Anton Lang is a potter, the *John* of 1910 was a plumber, the *John* of 1922, a builder. The principal actors range in age, from eighteen to seventy-two years.

A man of ninety has been known to sustain a part, but the majority of the actors appear to be men between forty and sixty. There is a tendency to keep the same rôles as long as possible, but certain characters must always be acted by young persons, since there is no make-up used—no rouge, no wigs, no footlights. Old men must take the part of old men, young men, of young men. *Mary* must always be a young unmarried woman; *John,* a young man. *Peter* may be older; but *Christus* must not look much older than the traditional three-and-thirty years. Josef Mayr sustained the part for three decenniums, 1870–1890, as Anton Lang has done from 1900–1922. Andreas Lang held the rôle of *Peter* for three successive celebrations, and since he is one of the best actors, in spite of his age he has been given the rôle of *Simon of Bethany* in the Play of 1930. It is said that he has played in as many as seventy different rôles, in the varied repertoire of the little village theatre.

Johann Zwinck, the Judas of 1910, held that part for three seasons. He had previously played the rôle of John twice, which represents forty years of acting. The stepping-down from important rôles to lesser ones on account of increasing age is the cause of much disappointment to these peasant actors. It is a very public reminder of the limitations of life, and has caused the untimely death of some of the most able of them. Josef Mayr broke down and wept, when he was made to feel that he could not continue as *Christus*. " I know," he said, " that I am too old for the part, but I had hoped that, in spite of all, you might still have left me my *Christus*."

Mayr was given the rôle of Prologuist and, later, made Bürgermeister of the village. But he died, three years later, never having recovered from his disappointment. Anton Lang has been given the part of Prologuist for the coming Play. No doubt he mourns the loss of his *Christus*, but he is a sensible man, has accepted the situation and made the prologue a living part of the Play.

Again: as no make-up is allowed, and seeing that the men and boys must represent the Hebrews of Judæa with long beards and flowing locks, they do not shave or cut their hair for about a year before performance of the Play, so that, for a time, Oberammergau is a village of long-haired men and boys. Most picturesque! But the day after the season is finished, the services of the village barbers are said to be in great demand!

To costume such a host of performers, is, in itself, a great undertaking, but no serious criticism of dress or colour scheme has ever been heard. The fact of all the costumes being made in the village, must not mislead any one to imagine them as being mere makeshifts. The most beautiful of materials are imported from Paris, Berlin, and even Damascus—brocades, velvets, embroideries and cloth of gold. Most of them have to be renewed for each season of the Play. All had to be made new—one thousand of them—for the Play of 1922, the old ones having been used during the war for bandages and needed articles of clothing. It takes a year to make these costumes, and the work has been done under the direction of Josepha Lang—a truly remarkable woman—with the assistance of twelve young girls. " Josepha has a sharp tongue," it has been said of her, " but she understands her business," which is very evident to those who have seen her unhesitatingly cut into the rich materials, with no patterns to guide her save the designs of her brother (Ludwig Lang, the remarkable director of the Play), and then have noted the exquisite results of her skill.

Josepha Lang was said to have been seventy-seven years old in 1910, yet she again superintended this work in 1922! Truly age did not debar her from her rôle! She died three years

ago, but like Dorcas of old, she will long be remembered, for the garments she made.

The brother, Herr Ludwig Lang, is now eighty-
four years of age, and can look back upon a life
of great usefulness. As head of the School of
Carving for many years, as Assistant Director of
the Play in 1890–1900, and Director in 1910–1922,
his has been a voice of authority in the great con-
cerns of the village, and to him much of the credit
for their success is plainly due.

Of necessity, much attention must be given to
material details in a village of less than two thousand inhabitants, which is preparing to care for
about twenty thousand people a week, for sixteen
weeks in succession.

A general cleaning, renovating and adorning
precedes the coming of the guests. The whole
village is swept and garnished, from stem to stern.
The great theatre must be renovated and painted,
and, this year, has been practically rebuilt and
enlarged. It is said to require a whole year to
repaint the scenery alone.

The houses of the village put on new coats of
glistening white, and retouch their frescoes; shutters are removed and unused rooms opened up;
downy feather beds and huge red pillows are hung
out to air; lace-trimmed curtains, sheets and other
company trappings are set in readiness; floors are
newly-painted, copper and pewter polished to a
high degree; and family portraits of those who

have sustained rôles in the Passion Play are hung conspicuously upon the walls.

The wood-carvers are busy, making great stores of toys and images, crucifixes and rosaries, with which to fill the shops and tempt the tourists, while unlimited supplies of photographs and postcards are arranged for. Plenty of garage space must be provided, for the automobile, kept out, religiously, before 1913, is now, of course, a welcome visitor. Railroad transportation must also be arranged, to say nothing of laying in food supplies for over three hundred thousand people during one short summer season. It would be strange indeed, if the material did not, at times, predominate over the spiritual, in the life of the Oberammergauers, during these months of preparation, and reports are always being circulated to the effect that they are commercializing their Play. But that they are earnest and steadfast in their refusal to do anything of the kind is demonstrated in many ways.

In 1873, for example, a proposition came from Vienna to remove the whole village to that city as an attraction in the great World Exposition. Here fame and money awaited, but the offer was at once refused. At the close of the Play in 1900, a company in New York offered five thousand dollars to each of the principal performers to take part in a play to be staged in that city, and this, also, was refused. Later, a deputation appeared in Oberammergau with the manuscript of the American play, *The Servant in the House*. The author, Charles Rann Kennedy, tells of the incident himself. The play was listened to with great interest, and a proposition made to Anton Lang to bring him to America, to sustain the part of *The Servant*, in a German rendering of the play. He was offered transportation for himself and family, a furnished house in New York with all expenses met, for the run of the play; in addition, a salary, most munificent from the point of view of an Oberammergauer, and a handsome bonus to the village. Lang was quite pleased with the idea, and brought the matter to the attention of the village council. Anton was informed that, of course, he was free to accept the offer if he chose, but that if he did so, he would never be allowed to play *Christus* in the Passion Play again. Whereupon, Lang turned down the American proposition, at once. Instances of this kind might be multiplied, and one other may be cited as being of especial value in showing the spirit of Anton Lang and his wife. In 1910, he and Mrs. Lang dreamed a beautiful dream of visiting Palestine after the season was over. Unwittingly, he mentioned this plan to a guest in his house, who was the head of a tourist agency. This enterprising individual delightedly included the Langs in his party, and soon it was advertised as a drawing-card that the *Christus* of the Passion Play would accompany that tour. The fact was commented on and adversely criticized by German papers. The *Christus* was commercializing his rôle! Finally the whole matter came to the notice of the innocent subject of the conspiracy, whose wise wife immediately went out and cabled a cancellation of all the arrangements.

As to the continued reports of the Passion Play being done into moving pictures, and the advertisements relating thereto, it may be said that there *are* films of Passion Plays, just as there are Passion Plays presented, occasionally, in different parts of the world, and, in some places, regularly. People do not, and, apparently, will not, distinguish between these and the Passion Play of Oberammergau. This Play has never been filmed, and, it is said, never will be. A letter from Anton Lang states: " Oberammergau has never been filmed as yet, so a great sum has been offered to the village and myself if I, alone, would take the part of *Christus* in a film arrangement."

" The Play could never be filmed as it is now acted," Frau Lang says. " My husband would be told to do this and to do that—what is it they say in the movies?—yes, register this, and that emotion. Until now, he has only acted according to the dictates of his heart and his spirit."

At the close of the last Passion Play season, it is said, moving picture agents were in the village, offering as high as a million dollars for the privilege of filming the Play; and the village was in the depths of poverty, at the time, owing to adverse economic conditions following the World War. This meant relief, it meant food, it meant comfort. Some of the younger men were momentarily tempted, but one of the older actors said decidedly: " If this Play is allowed to be filmed, I will go up to Ludwig's monument and, with chisel and hatchet, efface the inscription ('To the art-loving Oberammergauers, faithful to the customs of their fathers') from it." And Anton Lang said: "You'll have to get another *Christus*." Then these determined and loyal actors automatically prevented the proposition's being accepted, by betaking themselves to the barber's and being shorn of their locks! That settled it! The Passion Play could not be filmed exhibiting a cast of shorn and shaven actors! That night, Frau Lang says, she slept for the first time in *many* nights.

" No," say the Bavarian villagers, " in spite of our poverty, we will *not* play Judas to our tradition."

Naturally, a great deal of money is handled during the season of the Play, and speculation is rife as to the amount received and what is done with it. It is understood that all expenses are to be paid out of the gross income; of the remainder, a third is to go for village improvements, a third for the poor and in other helpful ways, and a third to be divided among the performers.

Up to the year 1800, there was always a deficit

Dear Mrs Swift!

I recieved your lettre of Oct. 3rd safely, and am sorry I could not possibly answer it before The report you mention is absolutely untrue, the play has not been commercialized and never will be, in fact it was this time actually a financial loss, prices for seats were absurdly low as were the charges for rooms and meals. I enclose report of the amount earned by the players for entire time spent on rehearsals and the play (nearly a year) and which by the time it was recieved was not sufficient to buy 2 pers. of boots with. ———————

Yours sincerely

Dr Anton Lang

to be met by the village community, and not until 1880 was there any appreciable profit to divide. Since that date, however, enough has been earned to make important village improvements, which include the hospital, the Carving School, and the straightening and widening of the Ammer, in order to prevent the yearly flood.

The performers, too, have received a slight compensation, rising in 1910 to about $625.00 for the highest paid actors, and decreasing to $7.50 for the children. Considering that this amount is paid for nearly a year of hard work, and only once in ten years, the Oberammergauers can surely not be charged either with extravagance, or profiteering.

The Play of 1922 was a dire financial disaster. It was the season of the depreciation of the German mark, which went down and down, and prices in Oberammergau were not raised in proportion, as keen managers, out for revenue only, would have raised them. Consequently, by the middle of the season, admission to the Play was costing five cents in good American money, and it was possible to go to the little village and receive two nights' lodging and five meals for as little as $1.50! According to the official financial statement, actors of the ability of Anton Lang received about $3.37½, as the mark was valued at the end of the season, while the net proceeds, to be divided among all objects, amounted to about $2,500.00!

As a consequence, the village faced a winter of

poverty and real destitution. In the fall of 1923, Frau Lang wrote: " Days are getting dreadful and many here, in the village, are unable to buy daily bread." On the day she wrote, a pound of bread was worth thirty-six milliards, a pound of meat sixty milliards, and a pint of milk thirty milliards!

It was to relieve such conditions that the delegation of Passion Play actors came to the United States, in the fall of 1923, to exhibit their village handicraft and to take orders for their work, there being no market for their products in Europe. This undertaking will be considered in a subsequent chapter, and the letter from Anton Lang reproduced on page 94 will further reply to the absurd charges brought against the Bavarian villagers of profiteering and commercializing their beloved Passion Play.

IX

THE PLAY: PERSONNEL OF THE PLAYERS

IN some capacity or another, practically all the villagers of Oberammergau are connected with the production of their great Play. Anton Lang gives the number of those who took part in the presentation of 1922, as being about eight hundred. Of this number, ten actors of the first class are listed, seventy-eight of the second, one hundred and seventy-two of the third, and two hundred and eighty-two of the fourth, besides young people and children.

There are less than a hundred speaking parts, but hundreds of persons possessing real artistic training are needed to properly and sympathetically take part in the great ensembles. The Entry into Jerusalem, for example, is not a mere mass of human beings. Although there are more than seven hundred engaged in the scene, each individual has his or her part, and enters into it with genuine understanding. Even the scene-shifters, the ushers, and the firemen in the wings, feel that their work is a necessary part of the perfect whole, and in this spirit carry out their duties.

The director of the entire vast production must, of necessity, be a peculiarly gifted man, and fortune has favoured this village in that such a man has always been forthcoming. Herr Ludwig Lang has already been mentioned in these pages. He succeeded his uncle, Johann Lang, who was Bürgermeister of the village for twenty-four years, the director and stage manager of the Play, and the instructor of the actors. He also held the rôle of *Caiaphas*, until his age and feeble condition made it clear, to every one but himself, that he could not continue in the rôle. Heartbroken at losing his part, he still continued as Director of the Play, until unable to stand without support. Finally, he was found outside the walls of the theatre, in a state of helplessness and heartbreak.

As one reads of the surprise and grief evinced by these players when their rôles are taken from them, it would appear as though the application of some system of retirement, at a certain age, would be a desirable procedure.

These players, however, cannot be measured by ordinary standards. In no other place in the world, probably, could old men be found, capable of really acting the parts of old men. That is one of the marvels of this Play, and of those who take part in it. Look at the photographs of these men of seventy and over—their wrinkled faces, their silvery hair and beards, their many marks of age and toil—and imagine such men utterly losing

JESUS WASHING THE FEET OF THE DISCIPLES

themselves in such characters as that of the Apostle Peter, or of Caiaphas, or of Herod! By some such process, one realizes the unique character of this community of actors, who have attained to proficiency in their art, as much by inheritance as by training.

Johann Lang was succeeded by his nephew, Ludwig, who, in turn, is followed by still another Lang, who is director for the Play of 1930. This is a young sculptor, Johann Georg Lang, whose name appeared as one of the village committee and as a member of the *Heimat-Kunst* (Union) during the visit to the United States in 1924. It is hoped, and indeed thought to be extremely likely, that the mantle of the elder Langs has descended upon this promising young man, for it is said that he is preparing some artistic innovations for the coming presentation of the Play.

The name of Lang must hold about the same relation to other surnames in Oberammergau as " Smith " does in many American communities. There were at least nine Langs in the cast of the last Play, some of them related and some not. Naturally, Anton is the man who comes most readily to mind when the name of Lang is mentioned. Probably there is no name of any living person, in the whole wide world, better known than his. The name of the man who sustains the rôle of *Christus* has, for the past thirty years, been finding its way into the consciousness of the entire world.

His face, photographed so often, and so strikingly reminiscent of the Christ face as conceived
by the Old Masters, has grown more and more
familiar with each succeeding year. The vision of
this face, framed in softly-waving brown hair, with
its kindly blue eyes, and delicately moulded features, will continue to suggest to certain types of
mind the ideal face of the Master. And men and
women everywhere will not cease to regard with
respect and affection the man who has imitated
in his life, and impersonated in the Passion Play,
the character of the blessed Lord. Anton Lang
is a native of Oberammergau, where he was born
in 1877. His father, Rochus Lang, was a potter, and the son has followed his father's trade,
which, in turn, he is handing down to his own
son, Karl.

Rochus Lang was an ambitious actor, and in
1900 reached his highest desire when he was
awarded the rôle of *Herod*. In 1910, however, he
was deposed, and played the part of a Pharisee,
although retained as understudy to the new
Herod.

It was the year 1900 that saw Anton Lang
elected to the rôle of *Christus*. The honour could
not have been entirely unexpected, for the old
Bürgermeister and Director had suggested to him,
some time before, that he had better go out
into the fields and try his voice, seeing that, some
day, he might be given a rôle. At this time he

was a tall, slender lad of attractive appearance, and fine character. In his youth, Anton had longed to be a painter, and it had been his delight to ornament his room, the stable doors and even the cow-stalls with his painting. He also had the imagination of a poet, and might have succeeded in literature, had the family finances permitted the necessary training. It was the custom, however, for the eldest son to follow his father's craft, and so Anton became a potter. Education he has surely acquired, for he has had opportunities to read and to travel, and has observed and thought to good effect.

Anton Lang married a most helpful wife. She was Mathilda Rutz, daughter of old Jacob Rutz, leader of the chorus in the Passion Play, and sister of the village blacksmith, who has so acceptably filled the rôle of *Caiaphas*. Frau Lang formerly sang in the chorus, and since her marriage has been busy in the rearing of her family of six children, and in the management of the beautiful home, the Pension Daheim, which is open to tourists. Before her marriage, Frau Lang spent some time in England and learned to speak English, which she taught her husband. They have been entertained in homes of wealth and social standing, and have travelled to Rome, to Palestine, to America. Frau Lang has also inspired a fine artistic quality in the work of her potter husband, which has been successfully exhibited, being awarded a medal of merit in the exhibition at Nuremberg.

Yet praise and admiration have left this simple village artist as unspoiled and loyal as he was when, as a sensitive youth, he heard the announcement of his election to the rôle of *Christus* with such emotion as to fall back, pale and lifeless. Lang is so wrapt up in his impersonation of the *Christus*, that he is oblivious to everything else during the days of the Play, keeping to himself in the room provided for him, and speaking to no one. He really *lives* the part he is playing, and suffers the agony he histrionically represents. It is said that, on more than one occasion, he has fainted during the enactment of the Crucifixion scene; for in spite of the best possible mechanical contrivances which are employed to lessen the strain, the twenty minutes spent on the cross proves a most trying ordeal. And in his refined, gentle, thoughtful, yet saddened expression, Anton Lang bears the mark of his thirty years' experience in this periodical treading of the *Via Dolorosa* —the Sorrowful Way.

With Anton Lang should be mentioned Josef Mayr, the *Christus* of 1870, '80 and '90. He, also, was a man of spotless reputation and lived his rôle, even expressing the wish that he might follow his Master and die on the Cross. Mayr was a man of great spiritual fervour, of the dark, Roman type—" the *Christus*," it is said, " of a

Velasquez, or a Van Dyck; Anton Lang is of the blonde type, such as Raphael loved to paint."

The mantle of these two remarkable men has now fallen upon a third *Christus,* Alois Lang, who has yet to be proved. He is a distant relation of Anton, but is of different type. He is thirty-six years of age and served in the World War. He is a wood-carver, usually pictured as working upon a crucifix, and is what is termed in the village a figure-carver. Young Lang is more of the type of Josef Mayr, with black hair and beard, and brown eyes. He is said to have a beautiful voice, mellow and appealing, which, of course, is a great asset. May he worthily uphold the traditions of his predecessors!

As already intimated, these Passion Players are often said to " live in their rôles." In the instance of the *Christus,* this might be held to be highly desirable, but how about the character of *Judas?*

In the village of the Passion Play, the rôle of *Judas* is a coveted one. In many respects it is the hardest part to sustain, and yet the most satisfying one. It offers an unique opportunity for an exhibition of the tragedian's skill, and affords scope for a variety of emotional effects. As a matter of fact, and when looked at from the viewpoint of dramatic ability, the best acting in the Passion Play has been done by the impersonators of *Judas.*

From 1830– 90, this rôle was handed down in
the Lechner family. It was played by Johann
Lechner in '30 and '40, and by Gregor, his son, in
'50, '60, '70, and '80. At seventy-one years of
age Gregor lost the rôle, and was so broken-hearted
that, in a frenzy of despair, he begged the committee on his knees to permit him once more to
have his *Judas*, and being denied, died, a few
months later, a disappointed, humiliated man.

Quite naturally, the rôle was coveted by Gregor's
son, Anton, teacher of drawing in the carving
school, and one of the most popular men and best
actors in the village. He was chosen as Prologuist,
however, a strenuous rôle, requiring a good voice
and retentive memory. This is the rôle to which
Anton Lang has been relegated, on being deposed
from the leading position as *Christus*. The words
of John the Baptist must often occur to these older
actors as they are called upon to step down and
aside, for younger men. " He must increase, but
I must decrease."

Johann Zwinck was the next *Judas*, a man who
seemed to have been created for the part in both
appearance and ability. At the time of his ap-
pointment he was very thin, with long legs and
arms full of nervous movement, a furtive expression in keen grey eyes, and a shock of dark, curly
hair, standing out in all directions—a very cari-
cature of a man!

He did some most impressive work—acting

worthy of the best professional traditions—in the rôle of *Judas*. Indeed, it is doubtful if one *could* be trained to represent the character of Judas as this man did, with his native artistic sense, and complete absorption in the character. After seeing Zwinck in this rôle, one spectator said: " I wouldn't meet this man for anything! . . . He must be the traitor he appears. It is all too real, too natural."

Yet by those who know him, Johann Zwinck has been called one of the gentlest of men. His secular calling is that of a decorative painter, which has never brought him any great success. This fact, and the loss of an invalid son, may have combined to strengthen the element of tragedy in his own life which affects and colours his acting. His representation of the remorse of Judas gripped the audience as almost nothing else in the Play. On one occasion, Zwinck, in his frenzy, nearly succeeded in hanging himself, and had to be rescued. Nor was this done for effect, seeing that the hanging takes place behind curtains. Like Lang, Zwinck never desired to be spoken to, on the day of the Play. " In my heart I am not Judas," he would say. " I must *think* Judas, and *feel* Judas, all day long, in order to *act* Judas."

For three successive decades, Zwinck held this rôle; but in 1922 it was given to Guido Mayr, another actor of consummate skill. In appearance, Mayr is a very different type from Zwinck.

He is short and rather stocky, and has a great mass of reddish hair and a short beard. His control of facial expression is remarkable, and a picture of him, depicting the gleam of avarice in his glittering eyes as he hugs his money-bag, would be worthy the brush of the greatest artist. Mayr was praised by all the critics for the remarkable acting he did as *Judas*, and the tragic heights to which he rose, at times, might well have been the envy of many a more renowned actor. Guido Mayr is a wood-carver, and could have been seen working at his bench in the 1924 exhibitions, an apparently timid little man. He is to sustain the *Judas* rôle during the 1930 season.

Those who visited the Players' exhibition in 1924 will be able to recall Andreas Lang, the fine-looking, elderly wood-carver, who diligently plied his craft, as the crowds stood around him. He has been called the best wood-carver in the world, and he has been an actor all his life. With his iron-grey hair and beard, sturdy figure and kindly expression, he attracted a good deal of attention. He was the *Peter* of 1910 and 1922, and expressed himself as desiring to continue in that rôle. He has contributed much to the welfare of the life of the village, and is one of its leading inhabitants. He is an enthusiastic mountaineer, loving outdoor life and sports. He lists third in his list of best-loved occupations—the first is his carving, the second, his play-acting—the long walks he is ac-

customed to take, the tramping he does through
the valley, or the skiing he does over the mountains. "As to travelling and seeing the world,"
he says, " that is not necessary . . . the whole
world comes *to us*."

The *Peter* of Andreas Lang was a most sàtis-
fying Peter—impetuous, impulsive, disloyal, repentant. Will Peter Rendl, to whom the rôle has
been given, play the part with equal vigour and
abandon? His family is a family of actors.
Thomas Rendl played *Peter* in 1900, having previously sustained the rôles of *Joseph of Arimathœa*
and *Pilate*. His son, Peter, took the part of *John*
in 1890 and 1900, and sadly relinquished the rôle
on account of age, in 1910, being cast, instead, for
Joseph of Arimathœa, whom he also impersonated
in 1922. And now, at the age of sixty, the rôle of
Peter is his. His alert, keen gaze gives assurance
of unusual power, and presages success.

The rôle of *John the Beloved Disciple* is, of
course, a totally different one. What versatility
is implied by the same man attempting the rôles
of both *John* and *Peter!* The former must always
be a young man, with the result that two seasons
are the very longest one man can keep the rôle,
and, usually, he plays it but once. It requires a
man of slender, youthful figure, and refined face.
The young Alfred Bierling, a plumber by trade,
made a most attractive *John* in 1910; and that he
felt the sacredness of the part is evidenced by the

way he received the announcement of his election. "I could work no more that day," he says. "I wanted to get away and be alone, where no one could see me, and I could see no one; so I went out of the village and into the woods."

Melchior Breitsamter, a young carpenter, tall, slender, and wearing a quite spiritual expression, played the part in 1922, and for 1930, Hanns Lang, a sculptor, who displays a good deal of character in his face, has been chosen.

Hans Mayr, son of Josef Mayr, the famous *Christus* of bygone days, is a man of great versatility. He has acted as Assistant-Bürgermeister of the village and as Assistant-Director of the Play, and played the part of *Herod*, in 1910. In 1922, he took the part of *Pilate*, and is to play *Herod* again, in 1930. He is a leading merchant in the village, as well as an image-carver, and is well along in years.

Sebastian Bauer was a most effective *Pilate* in 1910, and looked every inch an old and haughty Roman.

Hugo Rutz, the village blacksmith, is the scheming *Caiaphas*, the High Priest, while *Annas*, the older priest, is impersonated by Sebastian Lang. *Annas* and *Caiaphas*, in their gorgeous robes and with their supercilious expressions—two names that have come down in history as of those who instigated the plot which culminated in the death of the blameless Nazarene!

The women of the Play are a small group—
Mary the Mother of Jesus and *Mary Magdalene*
being the only two who figure importantly. The
legend of Veronica is introduced as an incident on
the way to Calvary, while Salome and two or three
others are included in this scene, and that about
the foot of the Cross. It is a fixed tradition that
these parts must be taken by young unmarried
women. Consequently, they are never taken twice
by the same person, for, in ten years, the young
woman would no longer qualify as young, and, in
all probability, would have married. Of course,
these young women lack experience, and suffer
greatly when placed in comparison with the male
actors, who have had the experience of several
seasons and many rôles. One of the few weak
features of the great Play is found just here—in
the women's parts. The voices are apt to be of
light timbre, and it is expecting a good deal of a
twenty-two- or twenty-three-year-old girl to enter
adequately into the sorrows and emotions of *Mary
the Mother of Jesus*. Nevertheless, there have
been some worthy holders of this rôle, notably
Ottilie Zwinck, daughter of the famous *Judas*.
She took the part of *Mary*, in 1910. She was somewhat older than the usual village maiden, was very
fond of acting and had sustained important rôles
in other plays. Her appearance was somewhat
matronly, and her face well suited to the character
of the *Mater Dolorosa*. She also entered keenly

into the sacredness of her work. "Ten years I had hoped and prayed," she said. "I had thought to myself, always, that if only I might have this rôle, I should want nothing more." During the summer of 1909, she was visiting in Munich when her father sent her word that if she wished to come home, she could have the leading part in a play which was to be given for summer guests. She consented to go, and threw herself heartily into the work. "Oh, how I love to act," she says. "It is my greatest happiness! . . . And when I played my part, people began to say, ' Here is the Mary for the Passion Play,' " as she, indeed, proved to be. But the one season was the limit of her career.

The *Mary Magdalene* of the same presentation was also a very attractive and artistic young girl, who ably sustained her part to the end of the season, when her dramatic career ended. This *Mary Magdalene*, however, Marie Mayr by name, married a German-American, and came to live in Chicago. She has given talks on the Passion Play, with great ability and charm, and has even attempted to produce a Passion Play in this country. She must have realized long since, however, that there is no village in America with three hundred years of play-acting bound up in its history, and that the peculiar spirit and genius of Oberammergau cannot be transplanted.

In 1922, Marie Mayr was succeeded by Paula

Rendl, daughter of Peter Rendl, a beautiful young girl of Germanic type with an abundance of flowing, blonde hair. The part of *Mary the Mother* was taken by Marta Veit, a small, shy, dark-haired maiden, with the face of a saint and an aloof expression. She was said to be very unsophisticated, however, and went about in her home between the sessions of the Play, helping with the housework just as any other young girl might do.

Anny Rutz, a twenty-three-year-old stenographer, has been chosen for the *Mary* of the 1930 season. She is a pale, quiet girl who, it is to be hoped, will rise to the exactions of her part. The *Magdalene* is to be presented by Hansi Preisinger, daughter of a village innkeeper, a merry-spirited girl, whose face shows character, and who is considered the best actress in the village. It is considered the greatest of honours to be chosen for these parts, and the choice can be regarded as constituting a real tribute to the character of the aspirant.

And now—the stage is set, the actors are assembled! It only remains to ring up the curtain and let the Play proceed!

X

THE PLAY: FROM THE PRELUDE TO THE ARREST

IT is a summer morning in the Bavarian highlands, and the entire Ammer range is touched by the rays of the rising sun, while away in the distance, the snowy peaks of the Tyrolese Alps gleam with the glow of dawn. The varicoloured greens of the forests take on a brighter sheen. The shining river reflects a hue of molten gold, and the grassy meadows fling back the shadows of the hills.

The Kofel raises its glittering cross to the sky as a signal, and a cannon booms from the heights above. From the belfry of the little church sweet chimes resound, and the quiet village nestling in its sheltered mountain nest, answers to the call of the day. It has a God-appointed task awaiting it; it must be about its Father's business.

Again the bells peal out their call, and, in answer, hundreds of homes are astir with the life of the new day and its sacred responsibility. It must have the blessing of God upon it, and so the church is sought at the very outset by a multitude of chastened, reverent actors, seeking strength for performance of the arduous task which is to be theirs that day.

A great multitude of guests, who have come from lands afar, to throng this Bavarian village to its last resource, is likewise astir, and restless with the thrill of high expectancy. A current of subdued excitement seems to charge the very atmosphere, and to communicate itself to every soul in Oberammergau.

The hour of eight finds hundreds of village actors assembled in their appointed places behind the scenes in the great theatre, and thousands of guests in their appointed seats in the vast auditorium. Their gaze is directed to an immense stage, stretched out before them, at the open end of the hall, through which they look out at the green hills behind the stage and the open sky above. Birds flutter about and perch themselves among the vines and greenery decorating the fragment of Jerusalem which the main part of the stage is intended to represent. The expectant silence grows oppressive. And, now, the eagerly awaited hour has come!

A muffled, martial overture, played by the orchestra in its hidden recess, strikes upon the ear. As it comes to a conclusion, two columns of stately figures appear at the back of the stage, advance with measured steps and take up their places in a line across the proscenium. The members of the Chorus wear white tunics and exquisitely-coloured, beautifully-draped mantles, of rich and gorgeous material.

The Choragus steps forward in the midst of the group, and sings the few lines which contain the sum and substance of the Play, as they do of the Christian doctrine of the Atonement:

> " '*I demand not,*' *thus speaks the Lord,*
> '*The sinner's death! I will*
> *Forgive him,—he shall live.*
> *My Son's own blood shall now atone for him.*' " *

The Chorus then divides, and falls back to either end of the stage, singing sweetly as the first tableau is shown in the covered, curtained pavilion set in the centre of the stage. This tableau represents Adam and Eve, clothed in white sheepskins, being driven from the Garden of Eden by the Angel with the Flaming Sword. Adam hides his face, but Eve looks longingly back to the attractive Paradise, where stands the Tree of the Knowledge of Good and Evil, with the Serpent hanging from its branches. Thus is represented the entrance of Sin into the world, but the Chorus, injecting a note of hope, sings:

> "*Yet from afar, from Calvary's height*
> *A morning gleam shines through the night.*"

---

* Naturally the text loses in beauty and force through translation. Especially in the choruses and prologues it is impossible to retain the strength of the German blank verse.

THE ENTRANCE INTO JERUSALEM

The Prologuist follows, proclaiming:

"Welcome to all, whom here the tender love
Of the Saviour invites . . .
Up to Him let us lift our thoughts and souls."

A second artistic tableau, representing God's remedy for Sin, " The Adoration of the Cross," is now staged. A group of beautifully-robed women and children are seen gracefully posed about a wooden cross, which a young girl, holding a palm branch, is embracing, while another figure kneels at its foot. The Chorus sinks to its knees, and softly sings a prayer.

Such is the prelude to the Passion Play. How can the great whole be adequately presented between the covers of a single book? It is a picture too vast, too complex for mere description. The most that can be done is to lift a few details out of their setting, and string them on a cord of imagination and memory.

The prelude is barely finished before a distant clamour is heard. Hosannas, growing clearer and louder, fill the air, while a great throng begins to pour upon the stage from all directions. On the surface, there appears to be no order; in reality, however, everything is carefully planned, and the final effect shows the highest skill in grouping and posing. The stage group finally numbers seven hundred persons of all ages—a most picturesque oriental gathering, exhibiting wonderful colour effects.

Hosannas continue to fill the air, palm-branches are waved, and garments cast on to a pathway opening toward the rear of the stage, along which a strange cavalcade is seen approaching. A majestic figure, clad in grey robe and red mantle, with wavy brown hair parted over a noble brow, a tender face, wearing a far-away expression, kingly in every line and contour, comes riding upon an ass! At the animal's head walks the young, fervent, delicately-featured John, carrying his staff, while the other disciples follow—a retinue of earnest, simple peasants, but, for the time being, actually embodying the physical presence and the spirit of the disciples of Our Lord.

"Hail to Thee! Hail! O David's Son!"

So sings the Chorus, and the multitudes echo the refrain, " *Hosanna to the Son of David,*" and again " *Hosanna.*" A group of eager, charming children, waving palm-branches, add their tribute, " *Hosanna to the Son of David,*" and " *Blessed be He that cometh in the Name of the Lord!* "

But stay! What have we here? The Temple is dishonoured! Here are traders with pigeons for sale, tables at which moneychangers are plying their trade, buying, selling, bargaining. Is it not written: *"My house shall be called a house of prayer?* . . . *But ye have made it a den of thieves."*

The majestic figure, fired with an indignation which evidences itself in his every movement, makes his way into the Temple precinct and proceeds to overturn the tables, and with a scourge of ropes to drive out the traders. It is the spark which starts the conflagration! The jealous, crafty priests find here just the pretext they need to justify their carrying out the purpose which has been gathering strength with the growing popularity of the Galilæan. These traders have been thwarted in their business—they have lost their doves, their money—and are the men who should seek vengeance. A little skilful prodding, a suggestion of reward, an appeal to their loyalty to their fathers—" Will ye, then, cease to be God's chosen people? "—will doubtless rouse them to resentment and reprisal.

The plot begins to thicken and take shape. The Sanhedrin is called to a night session, for there is no time to be lost. A tableau, staged at this point, likens their plan to the plotting of the brothers of Joseph, conspiring together as their brother draws near to the pit into which he is to be cast, clad in his coat of many colours.

The prologue explains how the

> "Serpent brood, leagued by the love of gain,
>   Seek with envy and spite
>   To bring Him to speedy ruin."

and the chorus sings variations on this theme.

The night session of the Sanhedrin is a spectacular gathering, assembled to bring a cleverly-planned scheme to fruition. Caiaphas, garbed in his robes of white and gold, and wearing his jewelled breastplate, presides, seated on a raised dais. On his left, is his father-in-law, Annas, wearing his self-righteous air, on his right, Nathanael, the silver-tongued advocate. Below are the rabbis in blue velvet robes, while scribes, Pharisees, and doctors of the law are grouped about the stage. An adroit argument is put into the mouth of Caiaphas. This Galilæan will stir up sedition and declare himself king. There will be discord and rebellion which will bring upon them the wrath of Cæsar, the armies to destroy the Chosen People and their holy law. Woe, woe! Something must be done at once! This upstart must be seized and imprisoned. *"In prison darkness He can let His light shine, and to the bare walls declare Himself the Messiah sent by God."*

But how is the plan to be carried out?

Nathanael brings in the traders—men with hatred and bitterness in their hearts. What have they to suggest? Caution must be used lest the followers of the Galilæan be aroused. Ah, Dathan has it!

"I know one of His followers through whom I could learn His whereabouts," he says, *" if I could offer him a suitable reward."*

Ah, Judas, thy reputation must have spread!

Hath thy love for the money-bags been noted?
Here is a member of the Sanhedrin who considers
thee susceptible of bribery!

So be it!

" Now we shall see who is to triumph," Caiaphas
exults. " This Man with His followers—to whom
without ceasing He preached love—or this horde
that we are about to let loose upon Him, filled
with revenge and hate." *

From the stormy session of the Sanhedrin in the
city, one turns to a peaceful family scene in the
nearby village of Bethany. The Master is meeting with His friends, and that it is a farewell visit
is indicated by two preceding tableaux: " The
Mother's Lament Over the Departure of Tobias "
(an incident taken from The Apocrypha), and
" The Bride in the Song of Solomon," gorgeously
pictured with her companions in a flower-garden,
lamenting, in the music of the chorus, the absent
Bridegroom.

The Lord and His disciples are warmly wel-
comed by their host Simon into the Bethany home.
Lazarus is there, with Martha and Mary, his sis-

---

* How these ardent, narrow-minded Jews—those chosen of
the Lord God from the beginning of the world—hated the
strange Prophet who went about doing good and preaching
love! His very presence was a profanation of their Temple.
It seems a very striking illustration of the dissemination
and leavening power of His Gospel that, *today,* the de-
scendants of the people who hated Him most and drove
Him from their synagogue, have turned over their Temple
for the weekly use of one of His worthy disciples.

ters, and Mary Magdalene. Love and confidence and hospitality warm their hearts. They beg Him to tarry among them, and refer to the storm of opposition in Jerusalem.

Is the Master's humanity tempted? Yes, but His divinity resists. " *Get thee behind me, Satan,*" He rebukingly says to Peter. " *The Son of man came not to be ministered unto, but to minister, and to give His life a ransom for many.*"

Then Mary Magdalene—the eternal example of " forgiven-much-therefore-loving-much, comes with her box of spikenard, very precious, and offers her costly oblation, with but one accompanying word —*Rabboni.* But in that word she conveys all the wealth of her heart's devotion, as she kneels and anoints the Master's feet, and wipes them with the flowing tresses of her hair.

"What waste!" says Judas. *"The ointment might have been sold for three hundred pence, and given to the poor."*

But Jesus, knowing well the false heart of Iscariot, commends not waste, but consecration, and canonizes the Magdalene forever with His spoken word: " *Verily I say unto you, Wheresoever this gospel shall be preached in the whole world, there shall also this, that this woman hath done, be told for a memorial of her.*"

The words are spoken which, much against their will, convince the disciples that the earthly kingdom of which they had hoped and dreamed is not

to be, and that some great disaster awaits their
Lord in Jerusalem. Yet they swear allegiance to
Him, and must needs go hence with Him.

Then comes the Mother. The sword must
pierce her soul, also. Never son had so sorrowful
a tale to unfold, never mother such dire need of
fortitude! She begs to go with Him—even unto
death. That would be easy. But to bid Him farewell—to send Him alone, on that journey to the
Cross—ah, for strength to do this, she cries aloud
to God.

Breathlessly and tearfully the thousands in the
auditorium watch this tragic spectacle, and a great,
universal sigh of relief speeds its passing.

The Master, His face set toward Jerusalem, and
accompanied by His (so far) faithful Twelve comes
nigh to the city. As Jesus looks down upon it
and realizes its mistaken attitude, its refusal of
the good, its certain progress toward destruction,
He breaks down in grief, and weeps over His
well-beloved Jerusalem. He foretells her doom,
and Peter and John and Philip again beseech
Him not to proceed thither, or else to crush His
enemies and establish the Kingdom of God
among men.

*"My thoughts are not your thoughts, nor my
ways your ways,"* He replies, and sends John and
Peter ahead, to arrange for the eating of the
Passover.

At this point Judas—calculating, careful Judas—

goes into conference with himself. He has been mistaken in this Master. *He* will never reëstablish the Kingdom of Israel, but speaks, continually, of parting and of death. He will have done with Him—he will withdraw, while yet there is time. The exact psychological moment, the chance to withdraw, is offered.

Dathan, the revengeful trader, comes upon him. " Friend Judas! " he begins, and adroitly draws out the misgivings which are forming in the mind of the disciple, concerning his prospects if he continue with his Master. Other traders gather around; they sympathize greatly. It becomes very evident to the mind of Judas that he must take steps to protect himself and better his present condition.

" The way to fortune lies before thee," is the parting word of the traders. " Whosoever will give information of the nightly abiding place of this Jesus of Nazareth will receive a great reward! "

"A great reward? " muses Judas, " that is worth listening to."

" Take courage, Judas, your future safety depends on this."

The Passover has been prepared in the " upper room." To foreshadow " The Last Supper," two tableaux are shown. They are marvellous portrayals, requiring four hundred persons, including one hundred and fifty children. The posing is

JUDAS ABOUT TO KISS HIS MASTER

most artistically done—a series of living pictures, ablaze with harmonious colour.

The first tableau shows " The Gathering of the Manna in the Wilderness," the second, " The Return of the Spies from the Promised Land." The colossal bunch of grapes they carry, requires the strength of two men to handle. Moses is pictured here with two gilt rays, like horns, rising from his brow, while the wilderness wanderers group themselves in artistic ensemble. The Prologuist links this bit of ancient history with " The Feast of the New Covenant," about to be established in the upper chamber.

The curtains then part, and disclose a striking semblance of Leonardo Da Vinci's conception of " The Last Supper." It is a scene of great solemnity, and by it, two important lessons are taught. The disciples, filled with longing for an earthly kingdom, and discussing among themselves the material preferment they desire to have, are taught by their Master the foundation principle of the kingdom He came to found.

" *He that is greatest among you let him be as least.*" . . . " *I am among you as one that serveth,*" He says, and thereupon passes from one to another, girded with a linen towel, and performs the menial service of washing their feet. Peter will not have it so. "*Lord,*" he says, "*Thou shalt never wash my feet!*" But later, in response to the Master's word: "*If I wash thee not, thou hast no part with Me,"* he impetuously exclaims: *"Lord, not my feet only, but also my hands and my head."*

" Ye call me Master and Lord," continues Jesus. *" If I then, your Lord and Master, have washed your feet, ye also ought to wash one another's feet. For I have given you an example that ye should do as I have done unto you."*

" The New Covenant " is then established by the passing of the bread and the cup, and *" Do this, in remembrance of Me,"* has remained a sacred duty in the history of the Church, no matter how differently the command and the sacrament have been interpreted. Both are given a forceful demonstration at Oberammergau, by a group of actors who reverently accept them as an everlasting covenant.

The feet of Judas are washed with the rest, and he receives the cup and the bread. But the hour for his part in the sad tragedy has at last come. With a meaning which both Jesus and Judas understand, but which is but dimly perceived by the others, the sop is covertly handed to him, and the whispered order, *"What thou doest, do quickly,"* is spoken. The traitorous disciple hurries from the room.

Those remaining protest unchanging devotion to their Master—through life and death. Oh, how tender the Master's heart, even though He must foretell the denial to be made by his vehement

Peter, within a few short hours! The matchless words of comfort, recorded by John, *" Peace I leave with you, My peace I give unto you,"* are spoken, together with the command to *"love one another as I have loved you,"* and the scene is over. *"Arise, let us go hence."*

Events now crowd quickly upon each other. A realistic tableau, showing Joseph sold by his brethren for twenty pieces of silver, precedes the picturing of the bargaining of Judas with the Sanhedrin and his exchange of the desired information for the thirty pieces of silver, and the accompanying flattery of the priests.

A current of sympathy runs through the great audience as Nicodemus courageously denounces Judas for his treachery, and condemns the action of the Sanhedrin; tokens of approval follow him and Joseph of Arimathæa who supports him, as they bravely retire from the place " where the innocent are put to death."

It does not take the great counsellors in the Sanhedrin long to argue from the proposed imprisonment of the Galilæan to the necessity for His death. The determination is soon reached— *" He dies—the enemy of our holy laws! "*

With Gethsemane now drawing near, a suggestive tableau is shown representing Adam and Eve at work. Eve is shown with a brood of small children, while Adam is sweating profusely as he labouriously strives to upturn the stubborn soil.

With great skill, the Chorus shows the analogy existing between Adam's sweat and the sweating of blood in Gethsemane, by the One who has assumed the burden of the world's sin.

Another tableau reveals Joab, the Old Testament captain, making ready to strike Amasa as he offers him a friendly kiss, while a part of the Chorus concealed behind Gibeon's rocks echo the sad tale of treachery, repeated in the infamous act of Judas—

> "O rocks of Gibeon!
> Cursed he, who his friend betrays
> With dissembling kiss of love."

The Master prays alone in the Garden, the disciples, near by, sink into slumber, while Judas and his escort are seen approaching in the distance. The fearful struggle between human frailty and divine purpose is depicted with heart-piercing reality.

The great Prayer of Jesus is introduced in the Garden scene, instead of in the scene of The Last Supper: " *Father, the hour is come; glorify Thy Son that Thy Son may also glorify Thee. I have finished the work which Thou gavest me to do. I have manifested Thy name unto the men which Thou gavest me out of the world. Holy Father, keep them through Thy truth. . . . Neither pray I for these alone, but for them also, which shall believe in me through their word, that they all may be one, as Thou, Father, art in me, and I in Thee."* . . .

Then comes the last, lonely phase of the struggle: the appeal to the puzzled and wearied disciples; the last remnant of hope, *"Father, if it be possible, let this cup pass from Me:"* the bitter realization that all human help has failed—*"Sleep on now, and take your rest"*—and, finally, the great momentous decision, *" Thy will be done! "*

An angel in shining apparel and with radiant wings descends, bringing the Master renewed strength and courage, and He sets His feet upon the Sorrowful Way, to falter no more.

XI

THE PLAY: FROM THE ARREST TO THE RESURRECTION

JUDAS and the Roman guard approach, and the kiss of betrayal is offered, accompanied by the salutation, *"Hail, Master!"* Events now follow in rapid succession. The disciples flee in terror. Jesus is bound, and led to Annas and to farcical trials, in all of which He conducts Himself with the indifference of a disinterested spectator rather than the anxiety of a prisoner fighting for his life. How truly is He " led as a lamb to the slaughter! " Yet it is not the attitude of a submissive coward that this Passion Play Christus presents, but the dignified bearing of a resolute soul, conscious of its rectitude and freedom from blame. The haughty priests obtain from Him just a single answer to their question. *" Tell us, art thou the Messiah, the Son of God? "* asks Caiaphas, and the reply is given, *" Thou sayest it, and I am."* That is enough. Such blasphemy is worthy of death. The Council must be assembled and pronounce judgment.

Meanwhile, in the outer court, two frightened,

disappointed men dejectedly cower. In pity, maids and guards invite them to warm themselves at the fire which is burning in a brazier set on the floor. This is the scene of Peter's denial of his Lord. Peter, whose vow rose above that of all the rest in promising loyalty unto death! Three times, in answer to the taunts of the soldiery, he denies his Lord! At last he turns, to see Jesus being led through the hall after His interview with Caiaphas. Peter meets a gaze of deepest sorrow, and in an agony of repentance goes out into the night.

The Sanhedrin goes through the form of summoning witnesses and conducting a mock trial. While it is in progress, a man, dishevelled, beside himself with grief and remorse, rushes in. It is Judas, the arch traitor, aroused to the awfulness of his deed!

The tableau introducing the despair of Judas, shows Cain awakened to the fact that he has slain his brother. It is an intensely tragic scene. Cain, tall and dark and stalwart, and clad in a leopard's skin, is dropping his weapon, a heavy tree-branch, and pressing his hand to his brow, where the murderer's seal is to be set. Abel, in a lambskin garment, lies dead, with an ugly wound in his temple. The background is of dark foliage, bold rocks and clouded skies, lighted by flames of fire, rising from a stone altar.

As the prologue explains, Judas' horror and

despair are a repetition of the experience of
Cain:

"Bitter remorse is indeed his portion,
And through the darkness there shines no ray of
hope,
'Too great, too great, alas, is my sin!'
Cries he, with Cain, the brother-slayer."

In an agony of fear lest he be too late, Judas
rushes into the midst of the Sanhedrin, crying
wildly: "Is it true? Have ye condemned my
Master to death?"

"He must die!" is the answer.

"Woe! Woe!" cries Judas, "*I have sinned—*
I have betrayed innocent blood!"

His ravings grow wilder, his railings fiercer.

"*Here, ye bloodhounds, take back your ac-*
cursed money!" he cries, tearing the bag from his
girdle and throwing it before the High Priest.
Then, with lamentation and curses, he rushes from
the hall.

Judas is seen wandering to and fro, fleeing from
the city, moaning and weeping in an agony of
repentance.

"O earth, open and swallow me up!" he cries.
"Master, the best of men—Him have I sold. . . .
I, detestable betrayer! . . . Must I still drag on
this life of agony? No, I can bear it no longer!
. . . Here, O life, accursed, here will I end thee!"
He unties his girdle—a blasted tree stands ready.

But, in the Passion Play, the realism of Judas'

JUDAS BARGAINING WITH THE CHIEF PRIESTS

end is pressed no further. Quite wisely, the final act of the suicide is left to the imagination of the wrought-up spectators.

Come now the trials of Jesus before Pilate and Herod. The prototype of the suffering Master in this experience is Daniel on trial before Darius, and condemned to be cast into the lions' den. The chorus expands the theme with telling effect.

Then appears the persecuted Prisoner, His hands bound and walking wearily toward the house of Pilate, the soldiers tormenting Him the while. The priests and scribes are here, as are the rabbis and traders. Pilate is summoned—a typical Roman in appearance, dress, and mental acumen. The flattering words of the priests do not deceive him, and he understands their hypocrisy. He is attracted to the Galilæan. He has heard good reports of Him, and does not propose to condemn Him on the charges of these fanatical Jewish priests. Moreover, a message come but now from his wife (who has had a warning dream) begs him to have nothing to do with this "just man."

Yet the wily priests are insistent. Every argument calculated to appeal to a Roman governor is put forward, even to the claim that the Prisoner is challenging the Imperial authority.

"*I admire your suddenly awakened zeal for the authority of Cæsar,*" retorts Pilate, with biting sarcasm.

The private examination of Jesus by Pilate follows. *"Art thou a king, then?"* asks the Procurator.

" Thou sayest that I am a king," replies the Galilæan. *" To this end was I born, and for this cause came I into the world, that I should bear witness unto the truth. Everyone that is of the truth heareth My voice."*

" What is *the truth?"* asks Pilate, enamoured of the words.

No; the Procurator decides that he will *not* condemn this just man to death. The Jews are greatly troubled. Are their plans to fail them, after all? One more attempt must be made!

" The whole people are stirred up," they declare, " beginning from Galilee! "

" Galilee! " echoes Pilate. " Has this man come out of Galilee? " Here is a loophole of escape! Herod, the king tetrarch of Galilee, is in Jerusalem; let him judge his own subject.

" On, then, to Herod," exclaims Caiaphas.

The pleasure-loving, sensuous Herod regards this as some new entertainment, arranged for his special benefit. Right gladly will he see this miracle-worker, and test His magic skill. Not a word can he draw from Him, however, and Herod regards Him as being merely a fool. The priests strive to win a judgment from him, but all he will do is to offer a white robe, with which to clothe this " king of fools." He simply refuses to be drawn into the pious quarrels of the Jewish leaders, and sends the Prisoner back to Pilate.

Once more the patient Prisoner is dragged to the house of Pilate by the chattering priests. They propose to coerce the Governor by threatening an appeal to Cæsar. At all costs, the Galilæan must be sentenced to death. They cannot do it, but Pilate *must*.

In sheer desperation, the Governor proposes to appeal to the people. It is customary to release one prisoner at the feast. There is a celebrated murderer named Barabbas waiting death in Jerusalem. The people shall decide between this man and the Nazarene. Barabbas or Jesus!

Now witness the priests' knowledge of mob psychology. The traders depart, each a different way, each to incite a crowd of idlers, ready for any new diversion. While the instigators of riot are busy without, the innocent Victim is led to the Prætorium, where all manner of contumely—the scourging, the scarlet robe, the crown of thorns—is heaped upon Him.

Out in the great auditorium, spectators avert their eyes from the painful scene. Yet the tragic magnetism of the story compels attention.

Soon Jerusalem is in an uproar. Crowds throng the stage as at the opening of the Play. Then, it was *"Hosanna to the son of David,"* with children's voices joining sweetly in the song. Now it is *" Crucify Him, crucify Him! His blood be*

upon us, and upon our children!" Pilate parries
the verbal onslaught of the Jews, and hot words
are exchanged between him and the determined
priests. At last, however, the uproar is such that
there seems no recourse but that he yield to the
people's choice. Barabbas is released, and Jesus
is led away to be crucified.

The chorus appears upon the stage in black
robes. Two tableaux are shown—" Isaac Bearing
the Wood for the Sacrifice " on Mount Moriah;
and " Moses Lifting Up the Serpent in the Wilderness "—a unique conception, carried out with
spectacular effect.

The stage is thronged with people on different
errands bent. A multitude follows Jesus as He
appears, drooping under the weight of a heavy
cross. Mary the Mother approaches, accompanied
by Mary Magdalene, John the disciple and Joseph
of Arimathæa. They see the mournful proces-
sion, and recognize its direful meaning. "*Oh,
where is any sorrow like unto my sorrow?*"
cries Mary.

Simon of Cyrene is laid hold upon, to help
carry the Cross. Other women appear, overcome
by poignant grief. As the Master passes her,
Veronica offers Him her handkerchief for His
sweat-covered brow, and thus the beautiful legend
of the Face forever imprinted on the kerchief,
finds birth.

As Golgotha is reached, ominous sounds are

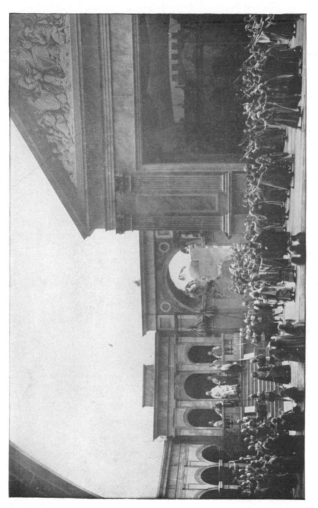

THE MOB DEMANDING BARABBAS

heard, coming from behind the scenes. A shudder runs through the great audience. Must it be witnessed—this indescribable agony? Cover the eyes if need be, but allow the soul to enter into the physical and mental suffering of this Son of God, willing to die for the love He bears to mankind!

The curtains are drawn aside, two crosses are seen, already erected; the third is on the ground. With difficulty it is raised to its place. *Ecce homo!* Behold the Man!

The details of the Crucifixion are carried out as the Gospels record them. The garments are bartered for, revilers hurl their taunts at the Crucified; the repentant thief is forgiven, the Mother is entrusted to the care of the beloved friend, the words from the Cross are spoken, the end comes! Yet it is *not* the end. If it were, well might the great company of spectators pass out of the auditorium, hopeless and utterly dismayed. But this need not be. "*Because I live, ye shall live also.*"

The body is taken from the Cross, in a scene which is a replica of Rubens' "Descent from the Cross." It is carefully entombed by loving friends; the tomb is sealed, a guard appointed.

On the morning of the third day, the stone is rolled away from the mouth of the sepulchre, with a peal like thunder. The guards fall on their faces. Jesus is seen for a moment, and then disappears. Mary Magdalene and other women come upon the scene, find the grave open and the Lord risen. The women hasten away to tell the news, but the Magdalene remains. Jesus appears to her, simply saying, " *Mary!* " to which she joyfully responds, " *Rabboni!* " " *Go to my brethren,*" says Jesus, " *and say unto them, I ascend unto my Father and your Father, and to my God and your God.*"

The final tableau depicts the Ascension. Christ is attired in white robes and surrounded by His disciples. Nearby are the faithful women. As He blesses them, Jesus slowly begins to rise. The movement, at first, is hardly noticeable. The assembled company follow Him with looks of adoration. As He reaches the centre of a great company of angels, the curtain falls.

Once more the Chorus takes its place in a semicircle across the stage, and jubilantly fills the vaulted hall and the heavens above it, with swelling pæan of praise.

> "*Hallelujah! He is risen!*
> *Hallelujah!* "

The Play is over, no one cares to speak, many eyes are dim, the great audience silently disperses.

The day draws to a close in the Bavarian Highlands. The setting sun drops slowly behind the shadowy hills, painting the encircling sky with its opalescent hues, and tipping with splendour the snowy peaks and forest-clothed hills.

The towering Kofel lifts high its gleaming cross into the heavens glowing with light, colour, beauty; and the heart of the beholder responds with hope, courage, worship.

"Praise, honour, adoration, power, and majesty, be unto Thee from everlasting to everlasting."

XII

THE PLAY AND THE OUTSIDE WORLD

FOR many generations the Passion Play has been guarded and preserved as their most precious possession by the people of Oberammergau. It has not always been easy to do this, and, at various times during its long history, foes without and fears within have jeopardized its existence. As described in a previous chapter, permission to present it had to be wrested from the State authorities almost by force. Then the village suffered severely from floods, at times, so that there was great financial stringency, and the Play was produced under great stress. As already related, the Play showed an actual deficit each year of observance until 1800, and until 1850, the performers received no recompense. In 1817, the great fire occurred in which the Passion music was consumed. It had not been published, and the composer, fortunately still alive, had it all to do over again.

There were also wars in which performers were called to participate, and when troops filled the village. The Franco-Prussian War broke right

CHRIST BEFORE PILATE

into the presentation of 1870, which was resumed in 1871. But no obstacles ever arose so apparently impossible of being surmounted, as those which confronted the villagers as they approached the year 1920, with its summons to the fulfilment of their vow. The World War was over, the Armistice had been signed, and crippled nations were gathering up the remnants of their national lives with new political alignments, and many economic problems. What was the situation in that remote Bavarian village, hidden among the Bavarian hills? Had it been able to escape disaster and conserve its resources? Not so!

Five hundred and fifty-five of its less than two thousand souls marched into the fray. Passion Players out to kill—what an anomaly! Sixty-seven of its men never came back, and many of those who *did* return, came home crippled and wounded. To be sure, this is the familiar story of hundreds of villages overseas. Each one invited sympathy, but in Oberammergau it meant something more than mere economic and physical disaster. Sadly the village council faced the situation and declared the fulfilment of its vow to be impossible—the only time in three centuries that this conclusion was voluntarily reached!

A personal letter from the Bürgermeister of the village, in reply to an inquiry about the Play, and translated from the German, reads, in part, as follows:

" Oberammergau 21 Juli, 1920.

"Answering your esteemed letter, we reply that a presentation of the Passion Play this year cannot be made, simply on account of the prevalent living conditions. . . . Because of the distressing conditions throughout all Germany the need is so great that it is not really living, and to offer the Passion Play to visitors would simply be impossible. . . . Oberammergau longs to present again the Passion Play.

"(Signed) WILHELM RUTZ."

This in 1920! Yet in 1922, the undaunted little village, displaying remarkable recuperative power, had rallied its forces, made the necessary preparations, and despite almost insuperable obstacles due to disorganized railroad facilities, difficulties in obtaining food supplies, and especially unstable money conditions, most magnificently presented its Play!

A statement made at this time and signed, " The Citizens of Oberammergau," has this to say:

" When we resolved to take up the Play again, we felt still bound by our vow and regarded it, as did our forefathers, as a holy duty. We are often reproached that the spirit of the vow is extinct, and that the Play is a mere matter of financial speculation. If that were so, we should surely not have taken the important step of resuming a matter which brings with it so much uncertainty and which might well prove to be our ruin. . . . The community is striving to produce the Play in a worthy manner, and to offer a pleasant home to their guests, but we do not expect to realize great

profit or riches. We cling to our traditions with faith-
fulness. . . . The Play bears the name, ' The Great
Sacrifice of Reconciliation on Golgotha.' So our forefathers christened it, and so also do we wish to have it
regarded and received. May it contribute to reconcile
every man to his God and to unite all Christian communities, and conciliate all hostile nations."

In round numbers, a quarter of a million spectators witnessed the Play in 1922, and, with very
few exceptions, rendered a verdict of approval and
wonder. From a dramatic viewpoint, it was a
splendid success, but from a financial standpoint,
it was, alas, a dire failure.

At the close of the season of 1922, the little
community found itself in a state of destitution
and suffering. Chiefly, the untoward situation
was due to economic conditions prevalent in Germany and elsewhere, which resulted in the closing
of the European markets to the product of the
Oberammergau arts and crafts. What did this
mean? With no other remunerative employment
at home, the bread-earners of Oberammergau
would be obliged to leave their village and seek
employment elsewhere, in order to keep their
families alive. In that event, what would be the
fate of the Passion Play? It could not be presented except, as it always had been, by an intact
community, one united in spirit and purpose. It
was a desperate situation for the Bavarian villagers, involving not only their Play but their very

existence. It was just at this time that repeated
offers came for the privilege of filming the Play.
Can any one appreciating, even approximately, the
temptation so steadfastly resisted by these people,
even so much as suggest their having desired to
commercialize their sacred possession?

The faith of the community in their God and
their mission proved to be not ill-founded. Outside interest and kindly co-operation found a way
out of the difficulty. Early in 1923, after about
three months negotiation between the villagers
and a number of sympathetic Americans, a contract was signed which resulted in bringing to the
United States a delegation of the Oberammergau
artists. Very few of the villagers had ever been
beyond the bounds of their own country. Imagine
the excitement occasioned when the proposal was
made that certain of their number, and these their
leading artists, should cross the Atlantic and exhibit their handicrafts in far-off America! It was
a tremendous adventure, but how would it coincide
with their tradition and peculiar mission in the
world? On the other hand, what fate awaited
them if they continued their struggle with hopeless poverty? Could they go out into the world
and still maintain their simplicity and sincerity—
still uphold the reputation of their village for
devotion to its unique tradition? Such were the
questions that were pondered and discussed from
every angle. A helping hand was outstretched to

them! Should they not grasp it? Finally, it was decided to do so, and a committee of the villagers was appointed, with Andreas Lang, Jr., as chairman, and including such familiar names as Guido Mayr, Anton Lang, Josef Albrecht and Georg Johann Lang.

It was also definitely determined that members of the delegation were not to present themselves as actors of the Passion Play, but merely as village craftsmen seeking new markets for the products of their skill.

With this idea, they immediately organized themselves into their *Heimat-Kunst* (Union) and one hundred and nine of the best carvers, potters, and other workers expended their best efforts, during the following ten months, upon articles intended to be included in the American exhibition. The men were paid for their work, thus bringing temporary financial relief to the village.

Meanwhile, plans were developing in America. Men and women of means and standing—financiers, actors, artists, authors, social leaders—who had been stirred to their hearts' depths by the Passion Play, were ready to have their names used as sponsors of the undertaking, and to underwrite, if necessary, the expense involved in carrying it out. An itinerary was arranged and reception committees were organized in the cities it was proposed to visit. The national chairman of the committee was George Gordon Battle, of New York;

with Governor Alfred E. Smith as honourary chairman, for the State of New York; John F. Hylan honorary chairman of the New York City committee; Addison Van Tine, treasurer; Elmore Leffingwell, secretary; Ludwig Nissen, chairman of the executive committee. Nationally known names were included in the list of sponsors, those of Burton Holmes, Frank D. Waterman, Royal S. Copeland, W. A. Harriman, Evangeline Booth, Mrs. Gutzon Borglum, Jane Cowl, Minnie Maddern Fiske, Ida Tarbell, Archbishop Mundelein, Rabbi A. H. Silver, Bishop W. A. Leonard, Newton D. Baker, Henry Turner Bailey, Judge Florence E. Allen, Lorado Taft, Jane Addams, and many others.

On November 8, 1923, Mrs. Anton Lang wrote:

" There are fourteen of our workmen coming over to hold an exhibition of our village work. It is all carvings, paintings, pottery and metal-work, as we have no trade market any more for our work in Germany. We hope to get new orders, for the future is very dark before us. Naturally, this will have nothing to do with our Passion Play, but we hope to save the future of our village by our work. Herr Lang himself will join the delegation, not as the Christus of the Passion Play, but as an exhibitor of his art work."

And, in a greeting to America, Anton Lang himself said:

" God's greeting to all those who have stretched out helping hands across the seas to us of Oberammergau.

. . . We have but one object in our visit—the most adventurous ever taken by people of our little mountain village—and that is to secure *work*. This work is for our families, so that they may be saved to carry on the crafts of Oberammergau and again present the Passion Play."

And the American committee announced:

" The fundamental reason for this exhibit is to establish in America an appreciative and permanent market for the exquisite work of the people of Oberammergau. . . . These men have become masters of their craft. Their crucifixes and altar groups have found their way into churches and cathedrals all over Europe. . . . We want to see American churches and American homes made beautiful by the carvings and ceramics that are second in fame only to the Passion Play itself."

The financial understanding was to the effect that thirty American business men were to underwrite the amount needed to launch the exhibition. The expenses of the workers were to be paid during the months of preparation, and the delegation of fourteen maintained during their five months' stay in the United States. Included in these expenses were the necessary costs involved in transporting the group and in providing four cars needed for the conveyance of their handicrafts from place to place, together with the cost of putting on the exhibition locally, obtaining the usual publicity and other incidentals. The gate receipts were to be devoted to the payment of expenses, and it was understood that neither the promoters nor the workers were to receive one cent of profit. The net receipts were to be used for the benefit of the village and of needy people, especially the children residing in the surrounding districts.

The fourteen craftsmen who made up the delegation to America were as follows:

Anton Lang (*Christus*), potter;

Andreas Lang, Sr. (*Peter*), carver (the most famous of his craft in the world);

Faust Lang (*Member of Chorus*), carver, second son of Andreas Lang, Sr.;

Emanuel Lang (*Money Changer*), father of Andreas Lang, Jr.;

Andreas Lang, Jr. (*Matthew*), carver;

Joseph Albrecht (*James*), carver;

Wilhelm Freisnegger (*Orchestra Leader*), carver;

Anton Haser (*Adam* and *Centurion*), sculptor;

Ferdinand Hochenleitner (*Member of Chorus*), carver;

Xaver Hochenleitner (*Roman Executioner*), carver;

Guido Mayr (*Judas*), carver;

Edmund Schmidt (*Interpreter*), carver (his chessmen are famous throughout the world);

THE SORROWFUL WAY

Ludwig Schweighofer (*Musician*), carver;
Benedikt Stückl (*Member of Chorus*),
carver.

The itinerary arranged included the cities of
New York, Cleveland, Cincinnati, Chicago, St.
Louis, Philadelphia, Washington, Baltimore, and
Boston. It extended over a period of about five
months, from December 23, 1923 (the date of
arrival in New York), to the latter part of April,
1924 (the date of departure from Boston).

The group of players departed on their journey
to the United States with the blessing of the Archbishop of Munich, which was expressed as follows:

" Munich, October 5, 1923.

"A delegation of the community of Oberammergau
intends, in a short time, to journey to America, in
order to conduct there an exhibit of their world-
renowned art, and by means of the orders and commis-
sions expected, to assure the economic future of
Oberammergau and, indirectly, the future of the Passion Play itself, as well. In no way is it sought to
profane the Passion Play, as the people of Oberammergau have hitherto, in lofty comprehension of their religious mission, declined every profit of a business-like
nature resulting from their fame. As Bishop of Oberammergau, I, therefore, gladly give my high pastoral
blessing on this journey to America.

" M. CARDINAL FAULHABER,
" Erzbischof von München."

A welcome awaited the Oberammergauers as
they steamed into New York harbour aboard the

S. S. " Reliance," December 12, 1923. It was attested not by the blowing of horns or the music of brass bands, but in the shape of published felicitations and expressions of interest from many well-known Americans, which are the possession of the Bavarian villagers to recall, and in which to rejoice.

A line or two from some of these expressions of goodwill will indicate the general feeling towards these guests from the village of the Passion Play:

BURTON HOLMES: "A hearty welcome to you all, and may our welcome be like yours to us, for you are past masters in the art of welcoming strangers to the world-famous village where you dwell."

JANE COWL: " For Oberammergau: The more I give to thee, the more I have.—*Romeo and Juliet.*"

IDA M. TARBELL: " Whatever they do seems to be simple, direct, honest, coming from within, and still untouched by imitation, greed or trickery."

MAXFIELD PARRISH: " When we welcome their artists and artisans from Oberammergau, may we also envy them a little; envy them their single, pure, happy interest in their art."

HERBERT (NOW PRESIDENT) HOOVER: " If we are
to secure increased production and increased
standard of living, we must reawaken interest
in creation, in craftsmanship."

JESSE LYNCH WILLIAMS: " It would be so easy
for these far-famed Players to get rich. The-
atrical managers have tried their best to exploit
them. But these artists will not produce the
Passion Play for money. . . . They prefer
making beauty to making money."

EVANGELINE BOOTH: " The Oberammergau Passion Players will unquestionably bring to us a
great contribution which cannot possibly be expressed in dollar terms, because spiritual values
elude or are above all such statements."

The truly great exhibition will be pleasurably
recalled by thousands. The Grand Central Palace
in New York, the Auditorium in Cleveland, the
Coliseum in Chicago, and similar buildings in the
other cities, were crowded with the various booths
housing the different exhibits. Not only was each
workman exhibiting his wares, but, the wood-
carvers, at any rate, were as busily at work in
their temporary shops as they would have been in
their own homes. It was exceedingly interesting
for the onlooker to watch the delicately-cut features or limbs or draperies emerge from the block
as the skillful artist manipulated his tools. The

artists were willing to talk, if addressed, but did not seek conversation. Great supplies of completed work were on display, each piece numbered and held as samples from which orders were received. Some of the altars or altar sections, baptistry fonts, mantels and pieces of furniture were large, and occupied considerable space. Of the secular pieces, the artistically carved furniture, especially that designed for a child's bedroom, attracted much attention; while the intricate, delicate, symbolic pieces of ecclesiastic carving were exulted over continually.

Great crowds thronged the exhibition halls almost constantly. Certain places, especially the section in which Anton Lang presided, were almost impassable, on account of the great multitude who wished to see this man and, if possible, grasp his hand and hear his voice. He was very gracious, if sometimes weary-looking, and, as he spoke English, many people were favoured with his greeting. The present writer was gratified to hear his pleasant assertion that she was " a missionaire of the Passion Play."

In Cleveland, Herr Lang mounted the stage and addressed eight thousand children assembled from the parochial schools. Thinking of the thousands of hungry children in his own land, he spoke feelingly of the blessings the children of America enjoy, and closed with these words: " You are the men and women who will guide this great nation, tomorrow. Prepare to shoulder the obligation and discharge it nobly. Above all else, obey the Golden Rule."

Figures as to the exact proceeds of their exhibitions in the various cities are not authenticated, but $65,000 is said to have been the sum of the receipts for the two weeks' presentation in New York; and in Cleveland the number of paid admissions for one day totalled 20,425, which give some idea of gross receipts and total numbers, if multiplied by the number of cities visited.

It is asserted that the Players carried back with them the sum of ten thousand dollars. This evidently caused some dissatisfaction in the mountain village, for the receipts were estimated to have been as high as $275,000. The Oberammergauers are only human, and those who stayed at home working hard for their existence may have felt a little jealous of their brother-workmen enjoying such pleasant times across the sea. Reports also reached them, as they reached many others, to the effect that the Players were presenting their Play in the United States. How natural an inference, and yet how incorrect! Consequently, one of their number was appointed to investigate the matter, Herr Benedikt Stückl, the chairman of the *Heimat-Kunst* (Union). The American committee was very willing to submit a financial statement, which showed that the village had in reality derived $100,000 from the

American trip, some of which would be forthcoming for future orders and sales. The charge
that the Play had been presented was, of course,
easily disproved.

In an undertaking of such magnitude, involving
the progress of fourteen individuals with four cars
laden with paraphernalia through the country from
city to city, during a period of nearly five months;
and these individuals, moreover, a company of
strangers in a strange land, it would be actually
impossible for the wheels always to run smoothly,
for plans never to " gang agley." As a matter of
fact, however, the expedition was strikingly free
from friction. One incident was widely commented upon, however, because of its occurring
in high places. Narrowed down to simple fact, it
appears to have been one of those unfortunate epi-
sodes for which nobody is really to blame, and in
which everybody associated had the best of inten-
tions. The publicity given the matter was, perhaps, its most unfortunate phase.*

---

* While in Washington, Mr. Ludwig Nissen, the chairman
of the executive committee, arranged to have the Players
visit the White House and meet the President. It was a
coveted opportunity, of course, and among the preparations
made was the writing by Mr. Nissen of a two-minute expression of appreciation for Anton Lang to deliver. The
President was reported to have cut short the programme,
and signalled for the Secret Service men to usher his guests
from the room. They were of course at a loss to understand
such treatment and were greatly embarrassed. The incident
was widely commented upon in the newspapers and Mr.
Nissen tried to explain. His speech had contained a reference to the sufferings of these people because of the " pecu-

And so the Bavarians came and went, leaving heartfelt expressions of gratitude to their American friends behind them.

Some of their comments are interesting. Said Andreas Lang, Sr. (*St. Peter*): " Your *Wolken Kratzer* (skyscrapers) are very *praktisch*. They provide light and air for thousands upon thousands to work in, and they are beautiful, too. They are the one really new thing in modern art."

" Oh, yes, we have seen much," said Guido Mayr (*Judas*); " we have been to the top of the Woolworth Building; we have been aboard the greatest of your battleships; we have even penetrated the sanctum of your great wizard, Edison. To me, your America is like fairyland."

From hearts touched and overflowing with gratitude, the delegation sent from Cleveland to George Gordon Battle and Ludwig Nissen the following telegram:

" We of Oberammergau, touched by the noble spirit and splendid generosity of the American people, pledge ourselves to erect in our village a monument of stone to be known as the American obelisk, upon which the

liar economic conditions " in their country, which he concluded must have been the cause of offense.

President Coolidge wrote a letter of explanation to Anton Lang, saying that it was "not permissible for the President to receive public addresses from people of other nations, except through diplomatic channels." Herr Lang undoubtedly would understand such an explanation, but Mr. Nissen felt that he should have been notified that the Bavarian delegation should be introduced by the German Ambassador.

names of those who have so generously received us will
be inscribed."

Anton Lang had the pleasure of welcoming his
wife to America. Frau Lang came for a short
stay only, and returned with her husband and
fellow townspeople. Many friends rejoiced that
she could have had this privilege, and no doubt
the opportunity afforded her to see other people's
ways conferred a great benefit upon her, in her
wise efforts to relieve the needy in Bavaria.

During the winter of 1925, Anton Lang wrote:

" Since our return home, our craftsmen have been
busy to work on the orders received during the time
of our exhibition in the United States. . . . Our tour
in the United States was a wonderful, never-to-be-
forgotten experience, and the love shown us everywhere
has been a source of uplift in our difficult task. . . .
Frau Lang and I have been much interested in, and
have worked for years that our old Passion-Players,
who became so poor during this awful war, should get
a home. At last our desire has been fulfilled, and a
pretty, simple home was opened just before Christmas,
thanks to so many kind friends and benefactors. At
Christmas we also dressed about fifty children, for
which our Woman's Club furnished the materials which
I was able to buy with the money I received for the
poor children while in America. These have been our
great joys at home."

Thus, to the everlasting credit of America, it
may be recorded that her generous aid, tendered

at a critical moment, furnished vital relief to the Bavarian villagers in their hour of need, and gave them a new incentive for future endeavour. And it did something more: it practically saved the Oberammergau Passion Play, for the benefit and spiritual uplift of future generations!

ADDENDA

ROUTES TO OBERAMMERGAU

THE village of Oberammergau in the Bavarian Alps may legitimately be visualized, at least during the Passion Play season, as the hub of a great geographical wheel with a number of converging spokes. These spokes indicate at least six important gateways to the hub, with a web of radiating pathways.

From London the gateway opens, from Harwich via Rotterdam, or Dover via Brussels, to Cologne and thence to Frankfort, Munich and Oberammergau.

From the northern ports of Germany there are direct routes—from Hamburg and Bremen to Würzburg and Munich; while from Berlin a short and straight pathway is followed through Leipzig to Munich.

From the east, Budapest and Vienna, the path is plain, almost a straight line to Munich by way of Salzburg.

From Rome and Venice a most picturesque approach is via Verona through the Austrian Tyrol and the Dolomites to Innsbruck, and up into

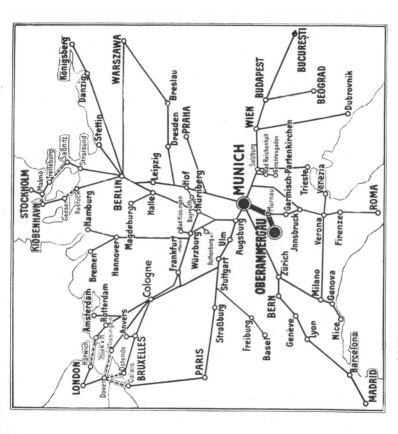

MAP SHOWING HOW TO REACH OBERAMMERGAU

the heights of the Bavarian Alps to charming
Garmisch-Partenkirchen, the Queen of Spas in
that mountain region; thence by rail or motor to
Oberammergau. This route may also be followed
from Milan, although a shorter trip from that city
is via Zurich direct to Munich.

Switzerland sends tourists over a scenic route
including the Falls of the Rhine and Lake Con-
stance to Zurich and on to Munich; or an equally
rewarding pathway may be chosen leading from
Lucerne via Zurich through the Austrian Tyrol to
Innsbruck, and thence through the Bavarian Highlands to Oberammergau.

The gateway from Paris opens into a pathway
involving a fourteen-hour ride by rail via Stras-
burg, Stuttgart and Augsburg, direct to Munich
and the Passion Play village. Of course, the route
may be varied by any number of side trips.

It will be noted that the approach to Oberammergau is usually made from the city of Munich,
the distributing point, probably, of nine-tenths of
the tourist travel. During the Passion Play season, in addition to the regular scheduled trains
from Munich with transfer at Murnau, special
trains (*Passionspielzüge*) will be run to and from
Oberammergau on the days preceding and following each performance of the Play.

Three methods of travel are available: the
usual reliable and satisfactory railway service;
luxurious motor travel over fine highways by pri-

vate automobile or de luxe motor coaches; and
the rapidly increasing use of the airplane, efficient
and safely-guarded.

By motor the routes are well-planned, numerous
and varied. From almost any city in any direction, motor busses or private automobiles carry
travellers to Oberammergau and the Passion Play.

From Munich numerous bus lines operate of
differing grades and differing prices. The Amt-
liches Bayerisches Reisebüro, Promenade Platz 16,
sends out busses at 9 A. M. on the day preceding
the Play for most delightful three-day tours; on
the first day going through the Isar valley, Mit-
tenwald, Garmisch-Partenkirchen, and Ettal to
Oberammergau; devoting the second day to the
Play; and returning the third day with a choice
of two plans. The morning may be free for sight-
seeing and excursions in the village and environs,
and the drive to Munich taken in the afternoon,
through most romantic mountain lake scenery. Or,
the return trip may start in the morning, and include a visit to the village of Hohenschwangau,
the Alpsee, and the famous Neuschwanstein castle,
all linked up with royal traditions.

For longer trips through the Bavarian Alps, to
the Dolomites, Switzerland, the Tyrol, and northern Italy, comfortable automobiles of the latest
makes, accommodating from five to seven persons,
may be secured at reasonable rates from this
company.

From the south also the approach to Oberammergau by motor over smooth, well-cared-for roads through the haunting forest-covered Bavarian hills, past charming old world villages to Garmisch-Partenkirchen in its picturesque setting at the foot of the Zugspitze, and then by way of Ettal to the Passion Play village, is an experience hardly to be duplicated in mountain travel.

Two motor tours from Heidelberg, offered by the Autobus Service of the Deutsche Reichpost in connection with the Passion Play, are delightfully planned. They are: The Scenic Route, from Heidelberg to Lucerne and return through the romantic Black Forest, with stops at half a dozen quaint old towns, including Karlsruhe, Baden-Baden and Triberg; and The Mediæval Route from Heidelberg to Munich and return, via the unique mediæval town of Rothenberg o. T. surrounded by its old stone wall, and the city of Nuremberg, of historic and artistic interest.

The Autobus Company of Cologne has planned tours of two weeks' duration, making a circuit of western and southern Germany with the Passion Play as its objective, and including fifteen hundred miles of motoring through the glorious scenery of the Rhineland, the Bavarian Highlands and the Black Forest, the whole region rich with the wealth of the ages in learning and achievement.

Thus the tourist approaching Oberammergau by one route and wishing to leave by a different way will find an almost bewildering variety of tours planned, from a motor trip of a few hours via the old monastery of Ettal, perhaps, or one or more of the gorgeous castles in castle-famed Bavaria, to extensive tours of any length desired; among the charming little lakes in their setting of tumbled hills; through the strange Dolomite region, and the Austrian Tyrol with its health-giving climate; into northern Italy; into the recesses of the Swiss Alps; or wandering from historic city to city, world-famed for music and art, up to the ports of the northern shores.

A map of air travel in Germany and the surrounding countries is an astonishing web of lines and circles representing air-ports and routes. From Munich, at least fifteen lines radiate in all directions. This method of travel is rapidly increasing in volume, and as an interesting way of reaching Oberammergau will undoubtedly be quite largely used.

For regular, dependable train service, of course the German Railways offer unsurpassed service. The German Tourist Information Office, of 665 Fifth Avenue, New York, has kindly provided a condensed time table of the principal railway routes from the usual points of departure to Munich and Oberammergau.

SUMMER TIME TABLE, 1929; NEW SUMMER TIME TABLE GOING INTO EFFECT MAY 15, 1930

Leave: Zürich .... 7:20 A.M.   1:37 P.M.   11:10 P.M.
Arrive: München .... 3:00 P.M.   9:15 P.M.   6:42 A.M.

Leave: Zürich .... 10:02 A.M.   7:43 A.M.
Arrive: Innsbruck (change) .... 4:26 P.M.   12:48 P.M.*   4:24 P.M.   10:25 P.M.
Leave: Innsbruck .... 4:40 P.M.   11:45 A.M.   6:40 A.M.
Arrive: Murnau .... 7:30 P.M.   2:39 P.M.   9:34 A.M.
Leave: Murnau .... 8:25 P.M.   10:50 P.M.   10:25 A.M.   9:45 A.M.
Arrive: Oberammergau .... 9:27 P.M.   10:50 P.M.   11:27 A.M.   10:50 A.M.
(Or leave train at Garmisch-Partenkirchen and take bus to Oberammergau.)

Leave: Paris Ost Bahnhof 7:15 A.M.   1:10 P.M.   5:50 P.M.†   7:50 P.M.   10:00 P.M.
Arrive: München .... 9:32 P.M.   6:35 A.M.   1:10 P.M.   10:54 A.M.   1:22 P.M.

Leave: Mailand (Milan) .... 6:25 A.M.   9:35 A.M.   6:40 P.M.   11:30 P.M.
Arrive: Innsbruck via Verona, Bozen, Brenner ...... 4:42 P.M.   7:30 P.M.   4:00 A.M.   8:50 A.M.
(From Innsbruck on, see time table above, or from Mailand (Milan) direct to München.)

* Only First and Second Class, only Tuesday, Thursday and Saturday.
† Orient Express, First Class only; only Tuesday, Thursday and Saturday.

Leave: Hamburg .... 11:25 A.M.   7:24 A.M.
Arrive: München .... 1:40 P.M.   9:33 P.M.
Leave: Bremen .... 12:03 A.M.   8:05 A.M.
Arrive: München .... 1:40 P.M.   9:33 P.M.
Leave: Mailand (Milan) .... 8:10 P.M.   7:10 P.M.   11:40 A.M.
Arrive: München .... 6:25 A.M.   6:40 P.M.   11:30 P.M.